The Curse

Ministering to the Hurts of Rejection

Jeffrey T. Hall

The Curse of the Bastard

Ministering to the Hurts of Rejection

Except where noted, the scripture comes from the:

King James Version (KJV) by public domain

Other Bible Translations include:

New King James Version (NKJV)®. Copyright © 1982 by Thomas Nelson. Used by permission. All rights reserved

ISBN- 13:978-1976425356
ISBN- 10: 1976425352

DEDICATION

This book is dedicated to the women of my life.

First to my Mother, Beverly Hall-Wightman, it was her prayers that kept me during the years that I was determined to kill myself.

Second to my Pastor, the late Naomi Hangsleben, it was her faith in God and in me that brought me to the full healing that I now experience.

Third to my wife, Libbie, it was her continuing love and forgiveness that helped build me up and encourage me.

Last to my daughter, Sarah: Her child-like faith has taught me to believe God for things beyond the realm of our own understanding.

FORWARD

The curse of the bastard makes one feels invisible and illegitimate. Though many experience the residual effect of this curse, those who were conceived out of wedlock and abandoned at birth may be overwhelmed by the way Satan takes advantage of that curse to kill, steal, and destroy. Help is on the way! My friend and ministry companion, Jeff Hall, has done the world, especially the Church, a great favor by writing of his struggles and final victory over the curse of the bastard.

He writes from the position of a wounded healer. Since he endured that curse for so many years, he has both the experience and the compassion to share the heart, the struggle, and the means to overcoming the curse of the bastard. As one who has "been there, done that," Jeff doesn't judge those under the curse. Rather than pushing them down through legalism or condemnation, he offers them a hand up.

As a minister of deliverance, I have witnessed the curse of the bastard at work as I have ministered hundreds of individual deep healing and deliverance appointments since the mid 1990's. People under that curse have a harder time finding God than those who are not under it. They struggle to identify their calling and often find it hard to hear God's voice and to receive and use spiritual gifts.

People under the curse of bastard feel like second or third-class citizens, even in the Church! That curse prevents others from seeing their needs or even noticing them! We ministered to one dear woman who was part of a small group in her church, but outside the group her fellow members didn't even see her when she passed them in a store. She would go forward in church for ministry and the ministerial staff would often minister to the persons in front and behind her and not even see her. Such is the curse of the bastard. She noticed a complete and immediate change in all her relationships when the curse was broken off.

One can't help but wonder if people under the curse of bastard are often wrongly judged as being "lukewarm," even though they often want to serve Jesus more than people who appear to be on fire for the Lord.

When you consider how many people were conceived out of wedlock, you realize how timely Curse of the Bastard is. Jeff Hall's Curse of the Bastard, will help deliverance ministers and the church at large to be more understanding and helpful to people who simply need help to understand why things are the way they are, and what must be done to effect spiritual change and reverse the curse.

When Jeff first asked me to write this foreword, I thought of Paul's words: "Praise be to the God and Father of our Lord Jesus Christ, the Father of compassion and the God of all comfort, who comforts us in all our troubles, so that we can comfort those in any trouble with the comfort we ourselves receive from God." 2 Corinthians 1:4-5 NIV.

God will use Jeff and *Curse of the Bastard* to release the comfort Jeff has received from Abba Father to comfort many who will be set free from the curse of the bastard.

Dr. Douglas E. Carr
www.dougcarrfreedomministries.com
His House Foursquare Church
410 South Clay Street
Sturgis, Michigan 49091

ACKNOWLEDGEMENT

The Author wishes to express his sincere thanks to Suzanne LeBlanc for her help editing this book. Without her help, it would not have been completed.

CONTENTS

Author's Introduction:

Some of the ideas you're about to read will probably make you to wonder if I've lost my mind, and I pray that they do. It's my hope and prayer that you doubt enough what I'm sharing to be like the "Bereans."

In fact, I challenge you to search the scriptures prayerfully, asking God to confirm the truth of what I've experienced. Ask God IF and HOW these truths relate to you personally and how they might relate to your family.

Since teaching this several years ago, many have shared with me what they too have experienced; many for the first time in their walk as Christians.

The following is typical of what others have experienced:

"Praise be to God, since the deliverance of the curse placed upon me by the sins of my parents, I now know true freedom, real strength, pure joy, absolute hope, the sweetness of forgiveness, and the fullness and power of God's faithfulness and great love. His mercy, love and holiness have touched me in a way that could not be comprehended by another person by mere words: It must be experienced. It is the most glorious and beautiful experience with the Holy Spirit since I was born-again. I cannot stop praising and thanking Jesus. For four full days since leaving I had not been able to pray. Praise and thanksgiving were the only things that seemed to come from my lips. My tears

of thanks spring from my spirit from morning until night...The peace of the Lord now manifest in my spirit and character is too evident to go unnoticed by those who know me well."

CHAPTER 1

My Early Years: Storm Clouds Arise

Acts 17:10-11 (KJV) And the brethren immediately sent away Paul and Silas by night unto Berea: who coming thither went into the synagogue of the Jews. {11} These were more noble than those in Thessalonica, in that they received the word with all readiness of mind, and searched the scriptures daily, whether those things were so.

Curses work in people's life to keep them from experiencing the fullness of **God's Blessings**. Jesus came into this world to destroy the works of the devil. Jesus came to free us from the curse so that we might experience the blessings.

When Jesus went to the cross it was to **exchange** all the curses for blessings. It is from the cross of Jesus that we today can receive the blessings of God. It was from Jesus' blood that was shed on the cross, and believing in Him that we can experience freedom.

He took our death sentence and gave us eternal life. He took our sickness and gave us health and healing. He gave us freedom from our sin. He gave us His righteousness for our unrighteousness. He gave us forgiveness and newness of life as a free gift.

Its only price is that we believe in Him and the sacrifice He made for us. There is not one person who cannot come to Jesus and receive new life. There is nothing a person can do that is too despicable for Jesus to accept and forgive him or her of everything in his or her past.

This is the story of a modern-day demoniac. This is the story of one man's search for freedom, a search for stability, a search to be free from the curse of the bastard. You too can be free, even as I was eventually.

I wanted to change the word "bastard" because it is such a strong word but God spoke to my heart that I could not. It's how God views it, and He intended it to be so. Being a bastard in God's eyes is one of the worst conditions you can be in.

Being illegitimate used to be frowned upon when I was growing up. Being illegitimate was something to scorn. Young, unmarried girls were sent away when it was found that they were pregnant. Today, because our society has changed so greatly if a woman is not married and has a child, it is hardly noticed.

In the sixties, the Supremes' song: <u>Love Child</u> mirrored the public's thinking about an illegitimate child. In our society today, we applaud the movie star who wants a child to rear, who has a baby through conception, even though she is not married.

As I have stated, being a bastard in God's eyes, is one of the worst thing a person can be. It carries with it the strongest curse in the Word of God.

Deuteronomy 23:2 (KJV) a bastard shall not enter into the congregation of the LORD; even to his tenth generation shall he not enter into the congregation of the LORD.

2 Corinthians 5:10-11 (KJV) For we must all appear before the judgment seat of Christ; that every one may receive the things done in his body, according to that he hath done, whether it be good or bad. {11} Knowing therefore the terror of the Lord, we persuade men; but we are made manifest unto God; and I trust also are made manifest in your consciences.

In 1985, I had a vision wherein I stood before Jesus at His judgment seat. I tried to explain to Jesus why I never did what He had called me to do. I tried telling Him how messed up my life was, how unstable I was. He was not the least impressed. At my left was a black man, whom I somehow knew had been martyred for his faith. I really don't remember the individual on my right, but I knew he had been martyred, also. So, my excuses about what kept me from doing what God had called me to do didn't appear very solid.

My heart's cry ever since I had rededicated my life to the Lord in 1978 has been for God to make me normal. I remember the prayer very vividly as I prayed: "Lord, I don't care what You ask me to do; I'll do anything You want. Just make me normal." It's been thirteen years since that prayer, and for the first nine and a half years that was my prayer, "make me normal."

In October of 1987, a friend at our church had a word from the Lord for me. Basically, it was that every tormenting spirit would lose its power over you if you would learn to forgive yourself. And if you've never walked in mental torment you have no idea what it's like, what someone with extreme torment goes through. It's a devastating experience. There was the feeling from when I was a young child, of being unloved, unwanted, rejected, extreme anger, depression, self-hatred, hostility, unstable moods and behavior, suicidal thoughts. These are but a few of the negative thoughts and emotions I experienced before being set free.

Suddenly God began to do some particular things that began to change me. That is what I'm going to share with you, some of the healings He has done for me. As with the demoniac that Jesus ministered to in the 8th Chapter of Luke's gospel, it happened very quickly.

One of the lessons that I learned at that time was there's no one way to define "normal" especially when normal tries to compare a Christian with a non-Christian. Normal has to be compared to a standard and our standard is Jesus. Jesus, I'm certain was not considered normal by any of the religious leaders of His day. Not even by the disciples or His apostles.

This man Jesus was different. He was strange to them because He was <u>The Standard</u> everyone else fell short of, and we Christians have to conform to That Standard. We have to conform to Jesus. So we can define <u>normal</u> as being Christ-like.

I have probably spent hundreds of hours counseling with my pastor and others. And we've counseled in many strange places, and things always got better, afterwards. In the first few years of my Christian walk, the Lord set me free from seven demonic personalities who would manifest themselves and rule my life.

I continued to get better; however, I could never walk totally free. Something always came and messed things up. Sometimes I felt a little like Job. When people would say, "All you have to do is make a decision. You don't have to be this way. Just make a decision." I kept saying, "You don't understand."

And that was the problem with Job's friends. They offered him good advice, good solid advice, but not one of them understood what was going on between Job and the Lord, and Satan. So, their good advice was useless to minister to Job's need.

16

That's kind of how I felt with all these friends saying, "Go make a decision." I made decisions left and right. I was making decisions everyday telling God, "I'm not going to do this again," and it still happened.

When I was preparing to teach this to our home Church, I first spent three nights with God. He kept dealing with me to share my testimony, not so much about the things that had gone on in my life, rather to share those things God had done for me. He kept speaking to my spirit man to share openly about my life.

One night, I finally gave up. I started writing down the things He was sharing with me. I don't like sharing all the negative things in my life; I would rather not do that but that's what God said to do, and I pray all this will minister to you. When I wanted to eliminate some parts, Pastor came up twice and said, "You need to do this for some people." So, I said to her, "Okay. I'll do that."

Basically, I'm going to share some negatives of my life. I remember some good times: fishing trips, camping out, vacations and other different things but they are dim memories. You need to understand what devastating effects curses can have on a person. I guess that's why God wants me to share these different things that have happened.

A fourteen-year-old eighth grade girl in Detroit, Michigan conceived me in 1952. My alleged father was sixteen years old. When I was born the doctors thought I was retarded, but I'm sure what they saw were the demonic spirits, particularly the spirit of rejection that was already active in my life.

I was adopted at a very early age, according to God's plan for my life by a couple from Saginaw, Michigan. But things in my early years were not right. By the time I was seven years old I was being psychologically tested in Ann Arbor, Michigan, where I shared that when I was in the first grade, we drove our teacher into quitting by the vicious things another boy and I did. I was a vicious little boy. We would throw spitballs at the teacher when her back was turned. Openly disrespect her to her face.

In the third grade, in 1958 or 1959, I received my first Bible for memorizing the 23rd Psalm. I grew up loving God's Word. I really didn't understand why, there was no understanding of it. I loved to go to Sunday School and to Vacation Bible School to hear more about God and His Son, Jesus. I still remember vividly hearing about David. A few years later in 1966, in one of my fits of anger, I ripped that Bible to shreds. I had been born again in 1964 and baptized in the Spirit and it was at that point that all hell broke loose. Satan unleashed an attack on

18

me that should have destroyed me. I literally am a "living miracle," today. I should not be here, I should be dead, or probably in prison for murder.

Early in 1966, my adoptive father, who was an alcoholic, flipped his car end over end nine times in a snowy field after spending the night out drinking. He was pronounced dead at of the scene of the accident, but my mother who was also born again and baptized in the Spirit called the Oral Roberts prayer tower. They started praying for my dad, and as he was cut out of the car for several minutes there were no signs of life, but he finally gave a gasp, and my father is still alive today! God is merciful; He answers our prayers. We still believe that God will save him some day. In December 1966, while my dad was still feeble from the accident previously described, I attacked him with a knife when he tried to take a belt to me to spank me. I was fourteen years old at this time and already weighed about forty pounds more than my dad. I could have killed him but God spared me from that.

I hardly remember more than this about those days of my life. Most of this time is nothing more than a blur to me today 50 years after the fact. I wanted so badly to have a normal life. I wanted to have a home life like my friends had. I hated my life. I hated my parents for what I felt they had done to me. All of the emotions during this time came out as hate and anger. I felt as if there was no hope of ever truly being like my friends.

All this time Mother and I had been going to Full Gospel Businessmen's Meetings. I loved going and had a great time. We also started attending Camp Furthest Out, and I experienced wonderful times with the Lord, but there was always some kind of warfare. I could not walk free once I got out of the environment of the meetings.

Violence and anger continued to grow in me. I saw more and more doctors. None of them had any hope, or any suggestions that really helped me. In December of 1966, I physically attacked my grandfather, (I no longer remember why), barely avoiding injuring him seriously. I was admitted to the psychiatric ward of the hospital for the first time that night.

I spent six months in a psychiatric hospital. Their recommendation was that if I went away to school I would grow out of it. It was a nice idea but it just didn't happen.

Shortly thereafter, I went to <u>Tennessee Camp Furthest Out.</u> Derek Prince was one of the principal speakers and it was my first experience with deliverance; I don't remember much except being prayed for in the large group; I do remember that part.

One morning in chapel, four of us were on our knees praying.

Several people separately came up front where we were and told us, "A ball of fire descended and stayed right over us, and eventually broke into four individual pieces. One piece went into each of us." I'm sure that in some form or other it was the Holy Spirit.

About that time, God called me to the ministry. I ended up running away from the call of God. I wondered how I can be a minister when you're so violent and so unstable. The first thing I did as an act of rebellion was to get married. What a mess that was! Can you image this 18-year-old child married, angry, frustrated? I made a mess of the marriage.

I joined the Navy, because I figured that was a good way to get an education. I certainly didn't want to be in the military, but I could not afford college. I thought going into the Navy and getting trained, as an electronic technician would solve some of my problems.

I received my electronic training through the Navy. I asked to be transferred to the East coast to avoid going to Vietnam. I no sooner reported to the ship than we got orders that we were going to Vietnam. I was tremendously afraid to die.

On the way to Vietnam, every night at the same time I experienced peace; this tremendous sense of peace just came over me. I couldn't understand what in the world was happening.

My wife lost a child, stillborn at eight and a half months, while I was on my way to Hawaii. I flew back home after receiving this news. I found that several of my friends (in the Jesus movement which saw millions of young people come to a relationship with Jesus through faith in His saving work), had been praying for me. Their prayer time was at the exact time, that I had felt God's peace on shipboard.

You've heard it said that there are no atheists in foxholes, and that's true. I was the closest to the Lord during the time I spent in Vietnam. I certainly was no saint. I would not have even considered myself to be a Christian. There was an awareness of God's presence but when the war was over that was the end of that.

When I got back from Vietnam my brother-in-law died of cancer. I really prayed that God would heal him; I knew the truth that God heals but when my brother-in-law died I turned to God and said, "I will never serve You again. I don't care what You do to me, I will never serve You. I will never have anything to do with You." I tell you today that THAT WAS A MISTAKE! You do not want to say that to God; He will put you through more than you will ever want to experience.

I always considered myself an agnostic. I couldn't quite go as far as saying I was an atheist because I have always had a healthy respect for lightning and that's not being fatuous. I always knew there had to be a

God; I just could not decide where He was, or how we related to one another. I was given a medical discharge because of my instability. The wife abuse grew worse; I continued to attack my wife. I do not know why she stayed with me.

We finally sought some counseling and tried to work things out. We worked on a few problems and then got into the area of sexual problems, and our counselor's suggestion for that was "Go start seeing some pornographic movies. That will help you." That took us into pornography and we got very involved, spending all our money. I was also on drugs and some alcohol at this time. These things all added up so that I had a very unstable job record. I had been fired from every job I had ever held nine, ten, or eleven of them. I don't even remember exactly how many. We had debt problems. If you don't hold a job, you cannot pay your bills. We had health problems; I was going to doctors and they couldn't figure out what was wrong. I literally was dying; I know that today. I lay on our couch when I'd come home from work, and I felt as if I was suffocating. It was hard to breathe night after night after night.

Finally, we lost everything, our house, cars, the whole bit. My wife decided she'd had enough and left. I was sitting at home one night and decided there was nothing whatsoever to live for. It wasn't just self-pity, that was true, but all that summer virtually every day I heard a voice whether it was an audible voice or inaudible I really don't know but this voice would say "Kill yourself, kill yourself, kill yourself, kill yourself..."

I had about a thirty-mile drive from the golf course where our league played. As I'd drive home this thing would say, "What's the bother? It's not worth it; just turn your car over and kill yourself." All my life the first time being when I was about 14, I have tried to kill myself even as a Christian there simply didn't seem to be a lot to live for.

Right after I had made the decision to kill myself, God gave me three visions. I know they were from God. I know God was trying to speak to me. The first vision was when I was a very young man and I was alone. I saw my death as a young man and there was no one to mourn me. No one even cared; it was just passing from existence. In the second vision, I was 75 years old; I saw the date on my tombstone very clearly. It was the year 2027. I saw my death; family, children, and grandchildren surrounded me. It didn't make sense.

The third vision I literally saw before I was even separated from my first wife; I saw my marriage to Libbie. I saw it as clearly as I experienced it the day we were married. I never saw her face but I knew she was a small woman. I saw the wedding dress she picked out several years later and I couldn't understand this.

Now I happen to have a mother who would not give up on me. I figured if I could get far enough away from Mom, I could get far enough away from God. Mom had a bunch of friends who wouldn't give up either and they prayed and prayed for me.

I would like to encourage mothers, particularly those who have sons and daughters who are not seeking God; do not give up on them. The thing that most impressed me about Mom's witness was that she never loaded up her gospel gun to blast away at me. That is not my mom.

When I would call her with problems she'd say the same five words to me, "Have you prayed about it?" I would scream, "You've got to be kidding me! There is no God. He doesn't care about me!" She kept saying, "Pray about it."

She sent me a book by Merlin Carothers, <u>Prison to Praise</u>. I read it and identified with each and everything in the book. I cried my way through it, and that night I said to God, "God, I've messed up my life royally! I don't know if there's anything You can do with my life. I do not know if it is over or not..." I was convinced that I was dying and said, "If you can do anything God, I'll do anything you want; just heal my mind." That was in 1978.

That fall, God miraculously opened the door to bring me back to

Michigan on my birthday. I got a call with an offer of a job. I packed things in my '66 Volkswagen station wagon and drove back with much prayer. My wife and I got back together, and Praise God! Everything's going to be fine!

Well, that was not quite how it worked out. My wife complained that I would never go to church, so I started going to church and that was wonderful! When I wanted to go to prayer meetings that was fanatical!

Things deteriorated in our lives and in April of 1979 she packed her bags and left. Within a week or so from the time she left I finally agreed to see a woman counselor and made an appointment. The day that I was to have the appointment, that entire day at work, a voice within me kept saying "If you go, you will kill her." When I got there, I was peaceful and calm. The demons were just speaking to my spirit, lying to keep me from going.

Fear was created in me because I knew how violent I was. I struggled with a multitude of demons, until we got there. After years of counseling and deliverance, (the process of expulsion of demonic beings), I slowly got better, but it was always a struggle. I struggled with depression, and every time I went into a depressed state I'd lock myself in my room.

When I first became a Christian, I spent a week locked in my room in my apartment. I would not answer the phone. I wouldn't answer the door. The police finally came out... I couldn't do anything through that entire time, until last summer, then, every time I went through a depressed state my spirit would sing songs to me. I hated it, I hated it for you want to feel bad and here's this song running through your mind and you can't turn it off. And it would go on and on. There is nothing you can do about it to stop it. I know it was the Spirit's way of ministering life to me during those times.

I continued having problems with guilt. I couldn't get over the guilt, the yo-yo Christian, up and down, up and down and up and down. We went to England to Bible College that went very well at first. In July of 1982, I was kicked out and we came back here. Again, I thought it was over; there was no way God could do anything with me. I thought I'd have to live this way for the rest of my life. But it really didn't work out that way. Just as a footnote, in 1985, the same man who kicked me out of Bible College sent me my ordination papers! He recognized something in us.

In February of 1985, I spent a month in travailing prayer. It is an extremely intense form of prayer which is much like a woman going through labor pains. I would go to work and come home at night but I do not remember what I ate or did. But I went up to my bed and cried out to God. "God, you have got to do something, You have got to do something." At the end of the month God told me my healing lay in the Fatherhood of God. I thought "oh yeah, mmm...that's nice." Nothing much changed.

In August of 1985, a friend said, "You have got to come down to this place in South Carolina and see it." Several of us packed bags and went to a convention. They had a banner on the wall that said, "God Our Father."

As soon as I saw that, my spirit leapt within me because I knew somehow during that week, God was going to heal me; God was going to bring to pass His word.

John Carr from Dundee, Scotland, ministered on "The Fatherhood of God." When he finished his message, they ministered to me in just a tremendous time of healing, but I found out I still wasn't whole. When I found out who my biological parents were, German and Polish, it was exciting to me! We ate perogies and kielbasa but it didn't make me anymore Polish than anything else.

In the spring of 1986 I suffered a mental breakdown. I do not know whether a psychologist would consider it a classical breakdown, but I collapsed. I could not function. Libbie and I separated for two weeks. When she came home one afternoon, I was buried under the covers. I couldn't come out. I couldn't speak. I couldn't do anything. To keep my job, they wanted me to get some counseling. So, I said I would and went to another psychologist.

I explained to him my feelings about psychology. I don't mind psychology but some people get really hung up about it. It has its place but it has never done me a bit of good. They told me I was manic-depressive, but they weren't sure. That is a big word for "You set these great big projects and when you can't do them, you go CLUNK! And it is one right after another."

It was about that time I said to God, "They have nothing for me." I made up my mind at that point that unless God healed me of whatever this was, there was no hope; I would die in that condition. I felt a little like the woman with the issue of blood in Luke Chapter 8. She spent all of her living on doctors and was still no better. There was no hope; God was my only hope.

In late 1985, God told us to move to South Carolina. We said we would do that, for we tried to be obedient to what God told us to do. We're not always going to be obedient in everything all the time, but when God says to do something, do your best to obey Him. He honors that in such a tremendous way.

We moved and were there for two days when I lost my temper

again, choking my wife Libbie unintentionally. It wasn't as bad as it was made out to be, but I blew up again. I was told I either had to leave the state of South Carolina, or they were going to call the police and have me jailed. So, I came back to Michigan while Libbie and the kids stayed in South Carolina.

One night while God was working out some things He told me I could deal with this problem as a cancer. I could go back to South Carolina and face my problem, which would be like surgery and would deal with the problem quickly. Or run away from my problem and allow God to heal it slower as in chemotherapy.

God did a wonderful work in our lives in South Carolina. It's been worth everything we went through, but I was still not whole. We came back to Michigan in March of 1987. Things went along well. We decided we were going to follow God no matter what. I thought I was healed.

May 30, 1987 came along and I blew up at a young man. I physically threw him out of my house, and that set off what was to be my lost summer. I don't remember much of that summer for it's a series of endless television programs and movies. The whole summer is a blur.

There was one night I was despondent, coming home. I had been very disappointed and had said life is not worth it. I was coming up

M47, just north of Freeland, Michigan when I tried to turn my car off the road and into a field and kill myself. I couldn't. Things got progressively worse. Things at home weren't going very well.

Libbie was under tremendous strain, tremendous pressure for a lot of reasons. In August of 1987, she had it. I don't blame her. We had a big fight. She moved out of the house. To me, it seemed like everything was over. I had really lost hope.

That summer was the first time I had lost hope that God was going to heal me. Libbie kept saying, "No, no. God is still going to do it." I told her I just couldn't believe any longer. We spent about a month separated.

After about the third week, it was amazing! It was the first time we'd ever gone through a real difficult situation like that and I hadn't turned inward. My normal response had been to take the phone off the hook, not talk to anyone and not answer the door, not go out of the house, not do anything. This time these things didn't happen and it shook me because I'm not used to responding like that. When the phone would ring, I'd answer it, but I still was not leaving my home. In fact, the only thing I did that summer was go with a friend to visit someone in prison.

After three weeks of separation, God said I needed to start doing something to exercise my faith. The only thing I could think of was to start back to intercession. I was living at my mom's house at this time. I started going to an intercessors' group at our church in Bay City, Michigan.

Once a friend shared a pamphlet with me that I'll be eternally grateful to her for, and grateful, also to the woman who wrote it. The pamphlet I was given was called; The Curse of The Bastard, by Gene and Earline Moody, and Glen and Erma Miller from the Lake Hamilton Bible Camp in Hot Springs National Park, Arkansas.

I knew that I was a bastard. Maybe there was something to this, so I took the pamphlet home to read. I could not believe what I read at first. I figured that God took care of all the curses; that could not be it. I still needed to know what Galatians 3:13 fully meant that Christ became the curse for me. The more I asked God about it, the more He seemed to confirm it. *Hosea 4:6 (KJV) My people are destroyed for lack of knowledge:* I was perishing. My life was wasted until God gave me revelation about the source of my problem.

Yes, this was a problem in my life, so I finally accepted it, accepted what it said, and by faith appropriated the message. Still nothing seemed to change.

After a month or so, suddenly, I realized things were not quite the same. There was joy in my life and for the first time there was peace. I realized the torment was gone. Everything was different! It was like all things were new, again. It was like being born again.

It was all very special to me when God delivered me and set me free from this curse! Most people who are born again are liberated, and their whole life changes. They get excited about that, and rightfully so, for that's the most important miracle they'll ever experience. My experience wasn't quite that way, but suddenly, I began to see things were new, things were different. It was as if I had been completely liberated. That's what happened. I was! But I didn't realize the extent of it.

CHAPTER 2

The Curse of the Bastard Defined

It was almost five months later that I had the opportunity to teach this in my church. You might think five months is not very long, considering what had gone on before in my life. But once you are free of that mental torment there's no way you can doubt. It is gone! It is gone!

And now I'd like to share some of the things God did for me during this time of my life. I am just one Christian God has set miraculously free, and if He did it for me, He'll do it for you! All you have to do is believe WHAT HE SAYS! Jesus said in John 8:31-32 *(KJV) if ye continue in my word then are ye My disciples indeed; and ye shall know the truth, and the truth shall make you free.*

I want to define the Curse of the Bastard, as I understand it and I have eight short statements. First, turn to Deuteronomy 23:2, *(KJV)* which says:

> *A bastard shall not enter into the congregation of the LORD; even to his tenth generation shall he not enter into the congregation of the LORD.*

As far as I know there are only two curses that extend ten generations, (See also Deuteronomy 23:3-4) (KJV).

34

> *"An Ammonite or Moabite shall not enter into the congregation of the Lord; even to their tenth generation shall they not enter into the congregation of the Lord forever: Because they met you not with bread and with water in the way, when ye came forth out of Egypt; and because they hired against thee Balaam the son of Beor of Pethor of Mesopotamia, to curse thee."*

I know we should not interpret the Word by our own experience, but for me to come to church was a struggle. I could not stand to come to church. I loved the fellowship. I loved to be in church, once I came... It was always warfare.

I remember the first few months we led praise and worship. Nobody knew if I would show up or not. Libbie lead worship alone more than we did together. It was always a struggle. To me, the congregation of the Lord means coming into fellowship with other believers. If it really goes beyond that, to me it really means being cut off from fellowship with God.

That does not mean you have no relationship with God. It does not mean you don't know God, or that you're not born again. Under this curse, trying to walk with God is a continuous struggle. It is always as if you're separated from God in some way.

The other thing I've seen about the Curse of the Bastard is that it attempts to hinder us from fulfilling the call and purposes of God in our lives. If I have anything on my heart, today, it is this. The time is so short before Jesus returns. I would love to see EVERYBODY come into what they are called to be in God. There is not a person in the world that God does not have a call and purpose for their life! And how much more so this is for we who sit in the church! God has not called us just to sit. Many times, we have said, "I'd just like to sit in a pew and not be responsible to God for anything."

I know that's not what God wants. I think sometimes our attitude, is that if we come on Sunday morning and sit in church we fulfill our responsibility to God. But it goes far beyond that, Church. God wants to demonstrate His love to the world, and He has chosen us to do it. Mark 15:16, Jesus says, "Go ye..." not "Wait ye."

People of the world do not want to see church. They don't want to see religion. They want to see the love of God. He picked us. He set us apart to do just that. It blows me away that God would entrust that kind of responsibility to the church!

That's what He wants for all of us, plus so many more individual callings. I cannot begin to tell you what God's called you to do as an individual; I'm only just now coming to understand what He's called me to do.

Since we have gotten free from this curse, God has shown us

some of what He has for us, and it's different than I've ever thought about doing. I will guarantee that!

The Curse of the Bastard attempts to destroy one's life. I can't say that too much! If this thing exists in your life, it will try to kill you, someway, somehow. It will use illness. It will use other people. It will use you.

I was so destructive. I cannot begin to tell you the dumb things I did! I wish I could use the excuse of being drunk or stoned on drugs. I was stone sober, and I would pull out in front of traffic because I was angry.

Four times that I know of I tried to kill myself in the car, and God would not let me turn the steering wheel. It was frozen. I am not a little man but I could not physically turn the steering wheel while going down the expressway at 80 to 90 miles per hour! The Curse will kill you if it can! It will use whatever means it can.

God's word says in Exodus 20:5, (KJV)

Thou shalt not bow down thyself to them, nor serve them: for I the LORD thy God am a jealous God, visiting the iniquity of the fathers upon the children unto the third and fourth generation of them that hate me.

I'm trying to define how widespread this thing is in America and in the world. What I see in the Word and in my prayer time as I seek God is that when this enters into a family it doesn't pass only from fathers to children, it moves through the WHOLE FAMILY! And you can have a brother, sister or a parent that you don't even know about.

It spreads like a disease through families, once it takes over. When we study the other ten-generation curse in the Word we can see it's considered to be an everlasting curse. And once this thing takes over a family it's so difficult to break.

There's no way to break it outside of the blood of Jesus. Once it starts it becomes so prolific that it takes over and keeps going. You can't make 10 generations without the blood of Jesus. You can't do it! It will happen again and again.

We're primarily going to look at David and his offspring. David's children were rotten. There is no other explanation, no other way to describe David's children. I cannot understand why a man who is called a man after God's own heart could produce such poor offspring. It does not make much sense. I know that godly parents in the Word do not necessarily mean godly offspring, but to have all the children listed as vile and evil, something's wrong.

God is very specific about the order in which He puts things in the Word. It's done that way for a purpose. You find that David's sin with Bathsheba and his causing Uriah the Hittite to be killed are followed immediately by seven chapters concerning David's children. How evil they were. How they turned from God, and how bad they were!

Different teachers use different translations because they like the way things are said in that translation. When I was going through The Scofield Bible, studying this, he lists II Samuel, Chapters 17-20, as the result of David's sin. That is why David's children were the way they were.

The next part of the Curse of the Bastard is that it does seven things in our lives in the way we respond towards God and towards godly things.

1.) The first thing is that the Curse of the Bastard causes us to be ambivalent towards God. Those were His words to me and I had to look up ambivalent. Ambivalence means simultaneous conflicting emotions, and boy! That describes it to a tee! One moment you love God and the next minute you cannot stand Him. One minute you love to be in His presence and the next minute you hate Him. Perfectly put.

2.) The second thing is that it causes us to be angry and hateful towards God. For 35 years I blamed God for everything. I had tried to rationalize that I was only a product of my heredity and environment.

For a period, I understood that if I forgave my parents, biological and adoptive, they must not be to blame. I had forgiven them for their role in my problems; therefore, they must not be to blame if I was still having problems.

I came to a point in September 1987; I finally understood that I was to blame for everything that happened. I thought for a long time my parents were to blame, my biological parents were to blame. There was only one other person I could blame and that was God. Everything had to be God's fault. I shortly realized that it was not quite correct. God said, "You need to be responsible for everything."

Yes, my parents made mistakes. Yes, things didn't go very well in my life, but, the thing that really produced the healing was when I could say" God I accept the responsibility for everything. On that basis, the Lord forgave me." Then God began to move.

3.) The third thing, which I see: both in the Word and in my own life is that it causes us to be fervently idolatrous. This curse causes you to have idols. It causes you to set up idols in your life and you love those idols.

I don't care if it's money, sex or power. One of the things I loved was cars. I loved fast cars. I could have set this up as an idol except I could never afford it. Another "idol" was my golf clubs. You say,

"Come on, give me a break." In 1978, I spent more time with my golf clubs than I spent with my first wife. It was a love, a passion to me. I worshiped my golf clubs. Like I said I am a little strange but I have learned it is not bad to be strange. It is bad not to be Christ-like. And that has brought a healing to me.

4.) Then the next thing is it causes you to be uncomfortable with God. Have you ever sat in church and just not felt comfortable? You could not really put your finger on it. What was the problem? You were just totally uncomfortable. I wanted to run out of more churches! And I ran out of a few, too. I could not stand to be in the presence of God, because it is so difficult to be in the Presence of God while under this curse. It stirs up the flesh and makes one want to either act out or run from His Presence.

5.) The fifth thing the curse will cause us to do is shy away from relationships. You are nurtured for nine months in the womb. There is a certain bonding that takes place between the fetus and the mother. For the most part, a bastard never has a father relationship. They have no relationship with a father as a general rule. There is no male bonding. With no male bonding, it is next to impossible to bond with God, with Father God. You cannot conceive of a father relationship. That relationship does not exist in your life.

6.) The sixth thing is that this curse separates us from God causing those under its control to fell deeply rejected. Not only from a relationship with God, but, it hinders us from having any close relationships with anyone.

7.) The last thing I want to share at this point is not something the curse of the bastard does, specifically. However, because it separates us from the presence of God, it will hinder us in these last days. We have been given a prophetic call. We will not get through what is about to happen if we do not experience the presence of God. And because the bastard keeps us separated from God's presence, it is going to be difficult, if not impossible, to get through this coming age, to walk a Christian walk, and have a Christian witness with the curse present in your life.

There is not much more I can say. I experienced God's presence throughout my entire Christian experience, from time to time. One time we led worship in Bridgeport; I do not know how to explain it, whether God physically took me out of my body and took me into heaven, or I just sensed the total overwhelming presence of God, but it happened. It devastated me. I just broke down. I do not know how long I was involved in that state but... It is not as if you cannot experience the presence of God. It is just that God's presence in our lives is the exception and not the rule. In four months from the time I was released from this curse until I taught it, I went from not being able to pray in the Spirit for more than a couple of minutes to being very easy to pray in the Spirit. When you are in a group of people and everybody is praying in the Spirit it is easy. When I was in my bedroom trying to try to pray in the Spirit it was a chore.

The week before I taught on the curse I started out in the morning with two hours of praying in the Spirit. I try to spend time throughout the day praying in the Spirit. Monday was almost one entire day spent praying in the Spirit and I never could have done that before. It is not that I feel any great, wonderful feeling. There has been a release in my life to experience God this way, to allow my Spirit to commune with God. It has been wonderful, Church. I do not know how I can tell you how wonderful it has been! For those of you who are fans of the original Star Trek, I know this is not a godly principle; however, it describes how I feel. Mr. Spock used to do this thing called a "Vulcan mind meld," and he would put his hands on the person's face. There was transference of thoughts. I wish I could bring you inside of myself and give you all the experiences of my life from the time I was conceived, until now. I've never taught anything I felt surer of. That has been more a part of my life. That has been more liberating to me. Go home and ask God.

When we get done teaching this we are going to go through the prayer of release. We are going to believe that God will set us free as a body and as individuals. You do not need me, to get free; you do not need your pastor, to get free. You need Jesus. It's faith, faith in Jesus.

In Acts, at one point it says Paul perceived the man had faith to be healed. You, too, can perceive and understand in your heart if you have God tell you this is in your life, and you can perceive in your heart, and you have faith to believe it. Believe it, and God will set you free. Why? Because that is who He is no more, no less. He wants us to be whole people. He does not want us to wait till we get to heaven. He wants to do it now, so we can demonstrate His love.

Music has always meant a great deal to me, even long before I became a Christian. And since I have become a Christian it has brought such healing to me. I do not think we have comprehended yet what music really does in the Spirit realm, and what a great weapon it is. What a tremendous healing it brings!

Let us reread Deuteronomy 23:2 again.

A bastard shall not enter into the congregation of the LORD; even to his tenth generation shall he not enter into the congregation of the LORD. (KJV)

In the first part of this book, I said the name of this would be

"The Curse of the Bastard." I wanted to change that, and use "illegitimate," but God said, "No, bastard is the correct word." It is a strong word. God intended it to be strong because it is one of two curses in the Word that extends to the tenth generation. And that is the way God sees it.

In the first part I shared a good portion of my testimony; how I've struggled from the time I was born, up until the first part of October 1987. I shared how I have struggled under this curse, how it has affected me, and what it has done to my life.

If I were to sum up what I shared in the first part in one sentence it would something like this; inwardly my life was 35 years of mental torment. Outwardly my life displayed anger, violence and erratic behavior. We went on to define a little bit about what the curse does, what the curse really is. The first and foremost thing about the curse of the bastard is that it separates us from God. It hinders our relationship with God. It says, "They shall not enter into the congregation of the Lord forever." There is a wall that the enemy puts up. This wall keeps us from coming into the fullness of our relationship with God. We also find we have a difficult time fellowshipping in church. We probably have a difficult time even staying in a church.

What I did not share in the first part was how and why I joined many different churches. I joined a church for their bowling league one time. All my life I have joined churches for strange reasons. Even up until last fall it was a struggle just to come to church and sit in church because of this curse. Once I was freed from it that was gone!

Another manifestation of the curse is that it hinders us from fulfilling the call of God on our life. The curse of the bastard attempts to destroy our life. Also, I see it as a four-fold way of how we respond to God and respond to the spiritual realm. We either become ambivalent towards God, which means we have tremendously, different emotions towards God, or we are angry and hateful towards God and bitter. We are always blaming God. We can be fervently idolatrous or we can just plain be uncomfortable with God and anything about Him.

CHAPTER 3

Scriptural Examples of the Curse

In this part, I'd like to go through the Scriptural examples about the curse and share a little bit from Scripture. The first thing I would like us to look at is Ammon and Moab, starting with Genesis 19:30-38:

Genesis 19:30-38 (KJV) And Lot went up out of Zoar, and dwelt in the mountain, and his two daughters with him; ... he dwelt in a cave, he and his two daughters. {31} And the firstborn said unto the younger, our father is old, and there is not a man in the earth to come in unto us after the manner of all the earth: {32} Come, let us make our father drink wine, and we will lie with him, that we may preserve seed of our father. {33} and they made their father drink wine that night: and the firstborn went in, and lay with her father; and he perceived not when she lay down, nor when she arose. {34} And it came to pass on the morrow, that the firstborn said unto the younger, Behold, I lay yester night with my father: let us make him drink wine this night also; and go thou in, and lie with him, that we may preserve seed of our father. {35} and they made their father drink wine that night also: and the younger arose, and lay with him; and he perceived not when she lay down, nor when she arose. {36} thus were both the daughters of Lot with child by their father. {37} and the firstborn bare a son, and called his name Moab: the same is the father of the Moabites unto this day. {38} And the younger, she also bare a son, and called his name Benammi: the same is the father of the children of Ammon unto this day.

If you look at this particular part of Scripture, it talks about the time immediately after Lot and his two daughters left Sodom and Gomorrah. Lot's two daughters were young women, neither of whom had children. They were afraid, because of the circumstances that they found themselves in, that they would never have children. Who is going to want us when they learn about our past?

They came up with the bright idea, "Let's go into our father, and we will lay with our father, and we can have children and rise up a name that way." So, they made their father drunk and they went into him at night. One daughter went one night and the other one the next night. They both became pregnant.

First, the oldest daughter bore a son and his name was Moab. Moab was the heir, the originator of the Moabite nation. The younger daughter had a son and named him Benammi, who became the father of the Ammonites.

If you look at Deuteronomy 23:3-4 they are also cursed with a curse of ten generations.

An Ammonite or Moabite shall not enter into the congregation of the LORD; even to their tenth generation shall they not enter into the congregation of the LORD for ever: {4} Because they met you not with bread and with water in the way, when ye came forth out of Egypt; and because they hired against thee Balaam the son of Beor of Pethor of Mesopotamia, to curse thee.

They are the only curses in the Bible I have been able to find that go on for ten generations. These two boys were both bastards. They were illegitimate, and then they ignored Israel when Israel came out of Egypt. Israel came to them and asked for provision and they said: "No, get away from us." They hired Balaam to curse Israel and God said, "No way, will you curse my people."

If you look at Nehemiah 13:1-2 you find that when the Levitical priest was reciting the history of the Old Testament, he read the particular verse, and instead of saying that it is a curse of ten generations, he said that it is an <u>eternal curse, an everlasting curse</u>.

> *Nehemiah 13:1-2 (KJV) On that day they read in the book of Moses in the audience of the people; and therein was found written, that the Ammonite and the Moabite should not come into the congregation of God for ever; {2} Because they met not the children of Israel with bread and with water, but hired Balaam against them, that he should curse them: howbeit our God turned the curse into a blessing.*

I wondered about that and said, "Why didn't they say it the same way?" I had understood it before as a curse of ten generations. I believe that without the blood of Jesus, you cannot successfully, keep everybody in a family pure through ten complete generations without someone falling under the curse, again. I think you can see by looking at all sorts of textbooks, that's the way it is. It just goes right down the family line.

The curse of the bastard caused the Moabites and the Amononites to withhold provision from others. You see that in Numbers 22:4 (KJV), possessiveness:

And Moab said unto the elders of Midian, now shall this company lick up all that are round about us, as the ox licketh up the grass of the field. And Balak the son of Zippor was king of the Moabites at that time.

I did not realize when I started reading, studying this out that it really deals with materialism; it deals with what God has been speaking to us about. The children of Israel came out of Egypt and said, "Let us have provision." And they said, "No, we are not going to give you anything."

The Curse causes us to seek ungodly confederations and occult practices.

Numbers 22:7 (KJV) and the elders of Moab and the elders of Midian departed with the rewards of divination in their hand; and they came unto Balaam, and spake unto him the words of Balak.

Numbers 24:1 (KJV) and when Balaam saw that it pleased the LORD to bless Israel, he went not, as at other times, to seek for enchantments, but he set his face toward the wilderness.

The Moabites were the nation who hired Balaam to come and curse the nation of Israel, and we all know the story. But Balaam also pursued occult practices. So, the Curse will also bring us into the occult and separate us from God, because the curse also motivates us to live under, and worship false gods.

Judges 10:6 (KJV) And the children of Israel did evil again in the sight of the LORD, and served Baalim, and Ashtaroth, and the gods of Syria, and the gods of Zidon, and the gods of Moab, and the gods of the children of Ammon, and the gods of the Philistines, and forsook the LORD, and served not him.

I went into a little bit of my background to examine some of the false gods I worshipped, and some of the things that were idols to me. We can worship all sorts of things. It's not just the religious things that we worship. It's the things in our day-to-day existence that we worship falsely. The curse will cause us to do that.

It caused the people to constantly be at strife with Israel, God's people, which is what I see happening today in the Church body. Being constantly at strife with one another over silly little things; things that shouldn't even be problems! If you look at the history of the Ammonites and Moabites, they are constantly at war with Israel for one reason or another. They led Israel into idolatry. It was a Moabite who was the first of Solomon's many wives and concubines outside of Israel.

The curse produces guilt by inciting lust. If you read in the book of Ezra, many of the people in Israel, many of the priests had married women who were not Jews. I thought that is not too bad. Then I began to wonder. Why weren't the Jewish women satisfactory to the priests? What caused them to look outside their own nation? These were the priests, the Levities, they knew better. They knew it was against God's law to marry outside the nation. God said to me as I studied this that it was lust. They looked around them and saw the same women day in and day out. They looked at these foreign women and they were more exciting to them because of lust. They were enticed, and it produced guilt in their lives.

The other trait I saw about Moab occurs in the Book of Ruth. We see how Naomi and her husband left Israel during a time of famine to go to Moab because they had heard there was bread in Moab.

> **Ruth 1:6 (KJV)** *Then she arose with her daughters in law that she might return from the country of Moab: for she had heard in the country of Moab how that the Lord had visited his people in giving them bread.*

The thing I saw here was that spirits, which work through the curse of the bastard, will entice us in the time of famine to depart from trust in the Lord. It's a seductive thing. It says, "There is no bread in your house. Come on over we have plenty to feed you with." But God says, "Just stay where you are and trust Me. I'll provide for you."

Let's look at David's offspring because they are the best examples recorded in the Bible to see the effects of the curse. If you were to teach on the family, David's family is not the group you would like to study. It constantly amazes me since I have been studying about the curse of the bastard as it relates to David and to David's offspring. How could a man like David, who is historically considered the greatest King the earth has ever known, produce the offspring that he produced to me is unfathomable.

It amazes me; I keep going back to the only reason I have been able to find. They understood that when the law said a bastard might not enter the congregation of the Lord to the tenth generation, God meant it, and they knew that. They didn't have to be reminded of that, continually. That is why it is not taught any other place, in the Bible, because they understood the law back then.

In David's children, we see the curse most clearly. The one thing that amazed me about David's children is their names. Israel named their children for special reasons. Abraham, of course we know was "the father of nations," and on and on and on. Names in Israel meant something.

All of David's children, who the Word talks about specifically, are the exact opposite of what they are named for. I think this is probably the best example of what this curse does.

I believe that when David named his first-born son, Amnon (which means faithful), he intended that to be his nature, or God had spoken to him that this would be his nature. Well it seems that Amnon was not a real nice guy. He raped his half-sister, and was killed by one of his other brother's servants.

The brother who had him killed was Absalom. The name Absalom means "father of peace," Absalom had Amnon killed. He led a revolt against David and committed adultery with his father's wives, and was finally killed when he was riding away from battle. His hair got caught in the branches of a tree. One of David's men came up and killed him.

There is not much in the Bible about most of David's children, his immediate offspring; it is as if they never existed. The reason, I think like we see in England, the further you get away from the throne the less is mentioned about them. They never did anything worthy of mention. Here they were sons and daughters of the greatest king of Israel, and they never did anything to influence their nation.

While I was studying, and praying about the story of David and Bathsheba which is found in Second Samuel 11:2f. David saw a beautiful woman, Bathsheba, bathing one night. He sent for her after learning she was the wife of another man. They had sexual relations and she became pregnant. After finding out she was pregnant, David had her husband Uriah killed. God said, "Look up the names Urriah." The name Uriah is a particularly interesting name; it means flame of Jah, which is the sacred name Israel used for Jehovah. God quickly spoke something to me. He reminded me of a story I heard. I cannot quote the exact story, but I think Uriah is a type of the church. Something we need to understand, particularly in this country. Something we have never learned about. God says in Hebrews 1:7:

Hebrews 1:7 (KJV) *and of the angels he saith, Who maketh his angels spirits, and his ministers a flame of fire.*

God meant that. I thought of the story I had heard about a young missionary named Jim Elliott, he was kind of a mystic, and I don't use the word in a spooky way, but, he had a special relationship with God. I believe it was the same morning when Jim Elliott and four of his friends, (who were missionaries to South America) were martyred, that Jim Elliott wrote in his diary, "God make me ignitable." That has always ministered to me. I am the kind of person who likes to wrap himself in asbestos. I do not like to be ignitable. The one thing about being ignitable is flames tend to burn themselves out very quickly.

I have the same idea I think most of us have, that my life is precious to me. I want to savor every moment of it. I want every moment I can possibly have. The one thing I am learning while I am becoming freer is to be what God has called me to be. In God's eyes, my life here only consists of what I can do for Him.

I do not know how much I can explain this but I would like to insulate myself a lot of times, but God says, "No, I would like you to be ready to spend yourself."

I got challenged about that when I went to the Soviet Union. I knew we were carrying in Bibles, I knew the Soviet Government, was not fond of that. I did not know exactly what would happen. When the Komitet Gosudarstvennoy Bezopasnosti (K.G.B.), the main security agency for the Soviet Union, started coming around and found several of us carrying Bibles, the situation became a little tense. At that point, I didn't even know whether we would be coming back out. God wants us to live our lives in obedience to Him. If Jesus had not been ignitable, He would not have of gone to the cross because Jesus knew what it meant to die, and what it would bring. He said, "I will gladly do it".

I was thinking about the Word my Pastor Naomi Hangsleben

read repeatedly to us.

>   ***Revelation 12:11 (KJV)*** *and they overcame him by the blood of the Lamb, and by the word of their testimony; and they loved not their lives unto the death.*

We do not live in a society, yet, where our lives are on the line. Maybe someday we might, or maybe God will call us to a place where our lives need to be ignitable. I pray mine is. I think that's something the church needs to know, particularly the church in this country. Our lives are not important outside of what we do for the Lord. They really are not. I used to spend months, years, trying to figure out why Naomi's husband, Emmott, passed away. Then I realized Emmott was ignitable. We get hung up over this thing about living 70 years.

>   ***Psalms 90:10 (KJV)*** *the days of our years are threescore years and ten; and if by reason of strength they be fourscore years, yet is their strength labour and sorrow; for it is soon cut off, and we fly away.*

We have a doctrine that says, "If one fails to live his full appointed 70 years that individual can't be a person of faith." God make us ignitable. Help us to understand that Jesus fulfilled His call in 33 years. Length of life has nothing to do when rating a person's level of faith.

Read about David's children and see they're all exactly opposite of what David called them to be. I'm going to make a simple statement and I will try to explain what God showed me; pray about it if you do not understand it. The curse of the Bastard appears to me (from both the Word and from personal experience), to affect men far more than women. That's not to say women don't come under the effects of the curse. I believe that God spoke to me while studying this that the curse falls on the man because God holds the man more accountable for producing illegitimate children. It is the man that must control his sexual drive in reproduction by limiting sexual intercourse to the confines of marriage.

CHAPTER 4

How the Curse Affects our Lives

"The judgment of God for the curse of the bastard, the judgment of God for women barring a child illegitimately is not on the woman, but on the man." When God originally said that, I struggled with it. Then He showed me how we have perverted our thinking. I'm talking primarily about premarital sex, how we've perverted God's laws of sexuality. We figure it is the woman's responsibility to take some form of birth control as a teenage girl, that it is not the male's problem, if she gets pregnant. Normally the girl gets pregnant and the guy walks away and is nowhere to be found. God says, "Because of the laws I established, I do not want you involved sexually, in the first place." Therefore, it is not the woman's responsibility but the male's. Generally speaking, teenage boys love to manipulate young women so they can have sexual relationships, "If you love me you would let me." I do not remember too many teenage girls coming up to a guy and saying, "If you really loved me, you would show me." It is the guys that do it.

I will get bold and say after marriage it switches. Sometimes women are the ones who at that point become manipulative using sex. God's way is spelled out in 1 Corinthians 7:1-4 (KJV). It says "Husband your body is not your own. It is your wife's. Wife, your body is not your own but your husband's." Our bodies are not our own; if you need the fulfillment it is your partner's responsibility to do that. We change everything around so. Men are judged because of their irresponsible cavalier attitude concerning sex and pregnancy.

It seems to me that there are 23 different ways the curse is manifested in the lives of David's children. I see these in the Bible when I examine David's offspring. I also saw these attributes in my life.

NUMBER ONE: SEPARATION FROM GOD

That is spelled out in Deuteronomy 23:2 (KJV):

A bastard shall not enter into the congregation of the LORD; even to his tenth generation shall he not enter into the congregation of the LORD.

Genesis 2:17 (KJV) *but of the tree of the knowledge of good and evil, thou shalt not eat of it: for in the day that thou eatest thereof thou shalt surely die.*

Genesis 4:11; 14; &16 (KJV) *And now art thou cursed from the earth, which hath opened her mouth to receive thy brother's blood from thy hand; Genesis 4:14 Behold, thou hast driven me out this day from the face of the earth; and from thy face shall I be hid; and I shall be a fugitive and a vagabond in the earth; and it shall come to pass, that every one that findeth me shall slay me. Genesis 4:16 and Cain went out from the presence of the LORD,* *and dwelt in the land of Nod, on the east of Eden.*

God's holiness demands that sin be judged. I've been reading a book by Rev. Sproul called "<u>The Holiness of God</u>." Get it, it is an eye opener! It has done wonders for me. God has certain standards, which we must call holiness, and there is no concept in our language to describe holiness. We have a difficult time understanding anything that has to do with holiness. It is so much more than purity. God's holiness demands that He judge all sin. When Adam and Eve fell, God told them, "If you eat of that fruit you will die."

I have always wrestled over that scripture. It is understood they died spiritually at the fall, which produced death. They were separated from God. I accepted that understanding for a long time but when I started studying this, God spoke to me and said, "When I said when you eat of that fruit you will die I meant it. That was My law, but I was merciful. In My mercy, I gave them their physical life, but there was death. There was separation and ultimately death. Because of My mercy I didn't execute the fullness of My judgment against them. I could have killed them on the spot but I chose not to."

You can go through the Word and see where God judges people and they drop dead. I have struggled over a God who would kill somebody. Was it Uzza, who touched the ark because the ark was beginning to fall and he dropped dead?

> *1 Chronicles 13:7 (KJV) and they carried the ark of God in a new cart out of the house of Abinadab: and Uzza and Ahio drave the cart. {9} and when they came unto the threshing floor of Chidon, Uzza put forth his hand to hold the ark; for the oxen stumbled. {10} and the anger of the LORD was kindled against Uzza, and he smote him, because he put his hand to the ark: and there he died before God.*

God said, "I have established rules and when My people violate them, the result is death. That's the way it is with the bastard. Our death is not so much physical it's spiritual. It's torment. It's being separated from God. I heard someplace that it was the greatest torment of hell. Hell would be a place where there was no presence of God, a total separation of everything that was godly. I have never really understood that until recently.

NUMBER TWO: EVIL IN YOUR HOUSE

> *2 Samuel 12:11 (KJV), Thus saith the LORD, Behold, I will raise up evil against thee out of thine own house, and I will take thy wives before thine eyes, and give them unto thy neighbor, and he shall lie with thy wives in the sight of this sun.*

Nathan came up and prophesied to David, "Because of your sin there would be evil from your house." I think if you live under the Curse of the Bastard, you know what it is to live with evil in your house. Idols bring evil in the house and people who worship idols become accursed, and God will not dwell with them.

2 Samuel 16:21-22 (KJV), And Ahithophel said unto Absalom, go in unto thy father's concubines, which he hath left to keep the house; and all Israel shall hear that thou art abhorred of thy father: then shall the hands of all that are with thee be strong. {22} so they spread Absalom a tent upon the top of the house; and Absalom went in unto his father's concubines in the sight of all Israel.

You cannot live in a house with someone who is a bastard, I believe, without knowing evil in some way or another, at some point. Some way this thing will manifest itself as evil.

NUMBER THREE:
GIVES OCCASION FOR THE ENEMY
TO BLASPHEME GOD

2 Samuel 12:14 (KJV), Howbeit, because by this deed thou hast given great occasion to the enemies of the LORD to blaspheme, the child also that is born unto thee shall surely die.

For years I struggled in my relationships and my walk, I knew it was my responsibility as a Christian to share my faith. My testimony was negated by my lifestyle that I showed because of this curse in my life. It was a struggle, because every time I would go to say something, the enemy would come to me and say "What are they going to think when you do something stupid? What are they going to think when you fly off the handle?" This thing kept coming back to me, how the enemy would keep coming to me and make a mockery of God. Here I am, supposed to be living a victorious Christian life, and I could not. I could see Satan standing in front of God just mocking Him, saying, "I know it happens with the whole church."

We see a good example of this in Job.

Job 1:1-12 (KJV), *There was a man in the land of Uz, whose name was Job; and that man was perfect and upright, and one that feared God, and eschewed evil... and a very great household; so that this man was the greatest of all the men of the east... and rose up early in the morning, and offered burnt offerings according to the number of them all: for Job said, it may be that my sons have sinned, and cursed God in their hearts. Thus did Job continually. {6} now there was a day when the sons of God came to present themselves before the LORD, and Satan came also among them. {7} And the LORD said unto Satan, Whence comest thou? Then Satan answered the LORD, and said, from going to and fro in the earth, and from walking up and down in it. {8} And the LORD said unto Satan, Hast thou considered my servant Job, that there is none like him in the earth, a perfect and an upright man, one that feareth God, and escheweth evil? {9} Then Satan answered the LORD, and said, Doth Job fear God for nought? {10} Hast not thou made a hedge about him, and about his house, and about all that he hath on every side? Thou hast blessed the work of his hands, and his substance is increased in the land. {11} but put forth thine hand now, and touch all that he hath, and he will curse thee to thy face. {12} And the LORD said unto Satan, Behold, all that he hath is in thy power; only upon him put not forth thine hand. So Satan went forth from the presence of the LORD. {2:1} Again there was a day when the sons of God came to present themselves before the LORD, and Satan came also among them to present himself before the LORD. {2} And the LORD said unto Satan, from whence comest thou?   And Satan answered the LORD, and said, from going to and fro in the earth, and from walking up and down in it. {3} And the LORD said unto Satan, Hast thou considered my servant Job, that there is none like him in the earth, a perfect and an upright man, one that feareth God, and escheweth evil? And still he holdeth fast his integrity, although thou movedst me against him, to destroy him without cause. {4} And Satan answered the LORD, and said, Skin for skin, yea, all that a man hath will he give for his life. {5} but put forth thine hand now, and touch his bone and his flesh, and he will curse thee to thy face. {6} And the LORD said unto Satan, Behold, he is in thine hand; but save his life.*

Satan kept appearing before God and saying, "Who is this righteous individual? Just take away everything he has and he will curse you. He only follows You because You have blessed him." God said, "No, he does not."

Job proved the exact opposite of what you see in the curse. Job never did curse God. His wife tried to get him to do that. His friends tried to convince him, but Job just hung in there and blessed God, even through everything.

NUMBER FOUR: DEATH

I think that one of the things that reigns supreme through the curse of the bastard is a spirit of death.

> *2 Samuel 12:14 (KJV) Howbeit, because by this deed thou hast given great occasion to the enemies of the LORD to blaspheme, the child also that is born unto thee shall surely die.*

> *1 Kings 2:24-25 (KJV) Now therefore, as the LORD liveth, which hath established me, and set me on the throne of David my father, and who hath made me a house, as he promised, Adonijah shall be put to death this day. {25} and King Solomon sent by the hand of Benaiah the son of Jehoiada; and he fell upon him that he died.*

We see through this curse, death, premature death, death through strange circumstances, on and on and on, death, death, and death. The thing that I struggled with the most is death. Working in a hospital was a glorious thing for me. It was a constant struggle. There is probably no place you are going to find the spirit of death more heavily than in a hospital. It was daily you battled with this spirit. The enemies told me all of my life, "I'm going to kill you, I'm going to kill me, and I'm going to kill you. One way or another I'm going to kill you." We see death being a struggle because of this curse.

NUMBER FIVE: SICKNESS AND INFIRMITY

2 **Samuel 12:15 (KJV),** *And Nathan departed unto his house. And the LORD struck the child that Uriah's wife bare unto David, and it was very sick.*

This is one I have never struggled with much, since I was saved. Before I was saved, I was literally dying. The doctors were not sure what was going on, but my body was falling apart because of sin. Since I have been saved it has not been a real struggle. I think of all the friends we know, the people we know, who struggle with different sicknesses and different infirmities and can never get free of them, never walk free of them. I begin to wonder "God, is that a part of this curse?" I think in a lot of cases it probably is.

NUMBER SIX: SEXUAL IMMORALITY

I want to say this is plain, simple, physical LUST nothing more, nothing less. It is the desire to be involved sexually for pleasure's sake, and nothing more. We will see a little bit later on when we look at sexual lust that it tends to lead to idolatry. I think there are two kinds of sexual lust, that which is just physical, and that which involves the spiritual.

NUMBER SEVEN: DECEITFUL LYING SPIRIT

2 Samuel 13:3-6 (KJV) But Amnon had a friend, whose name was Jonadab, the son of Shimeah David's brother: and Jonadab was a very subtle man. {4} and he said unto him, why art thou, being the king's son, lean from day to day? Wilt thou not tell me? And Amnon said unto him, I love Tamar, my brother Absalom's sister. {5} And Jonadab said unto him, lay thee down on thy bed, and make thyself sick: and when thy father cometh to see thee, say unto him, I pray thee, let my sister Tamar come, and give me meat, and dress the meat in my sight, that I may see it, and eat it at her hand. {6} So Amnon lay down, and made himself sick: and when the king was come to see him, Amnon said unto the king, I pray thee, let Tamar my sister come, and make me a couple of cakes in my sight, that I may eat at her hand.

This is the story of Amnon, David's oldest son. Amnon wanted his sister, Tamar, sexually. He went through all different methods to try to convince her to come in and lay with him. He had a friend called Jonadab, the literal Hebrew translation of Jonadab is Jehovah, meaning liberal. I think it is one of the biggest problems in the church, today, that we have a concept Jehovah is liberal, that Jehovah will forgive us for everything we do just because that is Who He is. Yes, He forgives us but He forgives us because He is merciful. He forgives us because we are under the blood of Jesus. Paul says in Romans 6:15 (KJV):

What then? Shall we sin, because we are not under the law, but under grace? God forbid.

This means just because we live under the spirit of grace it does not give us liberty to pursue all our desires. We have to bridle those. So Jonadab comes up to Amnon and says, "Hey, there is no problem. Just go lie on your bed and pretend you are sick. When David comes around, and asks you what's wrong tell him you are sick. Please have my sister Tamar, come and make me some food." Amnon said, "That's a wonderful idea." David came around and he told him this lie. David sent Tamar, and Amnon forced himself upon Tamar. It set in motion, again, all the effects of the curse.

NUMBER EIGHT: INCEST

Because of the same relationship I see incest as being a part of this curse

2 Samuel 13:11-14 (KJV) And when she had brought them unto him to eat, he took hold of her, and said unto her, come lie with me, my sister. {12} and she answered him, Nay, my brother; do not force me; for no such thing ought to be done in Israel: do not thou this folly. {13} And I, whither shall I cause my shame to go?

And as for thee, thou shalt be as one of the fools in Israel. Now therefore, I pray thee, speak unto the king; for he will not withhold me from thee. {14} howbeit he would not hearken unto her voice: but, being stronger than she, forced her, and lay with her.

NUMBER NINE: HATRED

2 Samuel 13:15&22 (KJV) *Then Amnon hated her exceedingly; so that the hatred wherewith he hated her was greater than the love wherewith he had loved her. And Amnon said unto her, Arise, be gone. {22} And Absalom spake unto his brother Amnon neither good nor bad: for Absalom hated Amnon, because he had forced his sister Tamar.*

After Amnon got what he wanted he hated Tamar. When one is under the curse of the bastard, it is easy to fall into hatred. When you struggle with rejection and forgiveness hatred is a natural progression. You end up hating yourself and those around you.

NUMBER TEN:
DOUBLE-MINDEDNESS, SCHIZOPHRENIA

I know by its psychological definitions you cannot claim this is schizophrenia, but look at 2 Samuel 13:15 (KJV).

Then Amnon hated her exceedingly; so that the hatred wherewith he hated her was greater than the love wherewith he had loved her. And Amnon said unto her, Arise, be gone.

You see a young man, Amnon, who loves Tamar with everything he's got, to the point he will lie, cheat, will do anything he possibly can to have her. As soon as he has her, he hates her. He is tossed back and forth, he hates her, he loves her, he hates her, and he loves her. If that is not classic double-mindedness I don't know what else it is!

NUMBER ELEVEN:

DEPRESSION AND INSANITY

2 Samuel 13:19-20 (KJV) And Tamar put ashes on her head, and rent her garment of divers' colours that was on her, and laid her hand on her head, and went on crying. {20} And Absalom her brother said unto her, hath Amnon thy brother been with thee? But hold now thy peace, my sister: he is thy brother; regard not this thing. So Tamar remained desolate in her brother Absalom's house.

Look at what happens to Tamar, David's daughter after she's raped by her half-brother. She spends the rest of her life in depression. She goes to her brother Absalom's house, and spends the rest of her life desolate. In reality, she is catatonic. She sits there and does nothing. She cannot do anything because of what she's experienced.

NUMBER TWELVE:

MURDER AND ATTEMPTED MURDER

2 Samuel 13:28-29 (KJV) *Now Absalom had commanded his servants, saying, Mark ye now when Amnon's heart is merry with wine, and when I say unto you, Smite Amnon; then kill him, fear not: have not I commanded you? Be courageous, and be valiant. {29} and the servants of Absalom did unto Amnon as Absalom had commanded. Then all the king's sons arose, and every man gat him up upon his mule, and fled.*

And 2 Samuel 16:11 (KJV) *And David said to Abishai, and to all his servants, Behold, my son, which came forth of my bowels, seeketh my life: how much more now may this Benjamite do it? Let him alone, and let him curse; for the LORD hath bidden him.*

Because of what happened, Amnon plots to kill his brother and eventually does. He is murdered. Murder is a prevalent way of death from then on through David's family. Also under that I see abortion, an attempt to cover up the effects of the sin through the hatred and murderous spirit. Abortion is also a part of idolatry. Do you see how the enemy creates a mess of interwoven garbage that potentiates the root curse of the Bastard?

NUMBER THIRTEEN: BROKEN RELATIONSHIPS

2 Samuel 13:34&35&37 (KJV) *But Absalom fled... kings' sons come: as thy servant said, so it is. {37} But Absalom fled, and went to Talmai, the son of Ammihud, king of Geshur. And David mourned for his son every day.*

Because of Absalom's murdering his brother, a spirit of guilt causes him to flee from his father, David. They spend the rest of their days having no relationship. Absalom was the son David loved supremely. Look at how David responds to this whole experience with Absalom. He always responds lovingly, even to the point at times of going overboard.

I think that is the example of the relationship with God and us regarding the curse of the Bastard. God loves us supremely. He loves us with an undying love, an unselfish love, an agape love, but we cannot understand, we cannot comprehend this kind of love that is willing to forgive, so, we try to run from God, continuously. We find it difficult to develop a relationship with God. The curse is often visible in lack of any genuine relationships.

NUMBER FOURTEEN: SELF-PROMOTING

__2 Samuel 15:1-6 (KJV)__ Absalom prepared him chariots and horses, and fifty men to run before him. {2} And Absalom rose up early, and stood beside the way of the gate: and it was so, that when any man that had a controversy came to the king for judgment, then Absalom called unto him, and said, Of what city *art thou? And he said, Thy servant is of one of the tribes of Israel. {3} And Absalom said unto him, See, thy matters are good and right; but there is no man deputed of the king to hear thee. {4} Absalom said moreover, Oh that I were made judge in the land, that every man which hath any suit or cause might come unto me, and I would do him justice! {5} and it was so, that when any man came nigh to him to do him obeisance, he put forth his hand, and took him, and kissed him. {6} and on this manner did Absalom to all Israel that came to the king for judgment: so Absalom stole the hearts of the men of Israel.*

After a period in exile Absalom decides he has a word from God or something, "I am going to be King." Absalom takes it upon himself to promote himself to be King. He starts attracting all the dissatisfied, all the unsatisfied, all the people who have problems with David. He says, "Come follow me I will take care of you." But soon Absalom, wanting to be king, spends the rest of his brief life hunting down and trying to kill his father, King David.

When I saw that, the first thing that came to my mind was, it has a "dealership's general manager," and this guy is going on miles and miles and miles an hour with his mouth. This is the same thing I see in Absalom. Promoting himself. Trying to sell himself, haughty, a haughty spirit. This is what he becomes.

I think we do it in the church. In some ways, I used to do it. "Hey, you don't like so and so. Come on over. Let me talk to you a little bit. How many churches have split because of somebody doing something like this! You get a small division in a church and instead of working things out scripturally, "Hey, come on let's go over here, and we will start our own church!" God help us!

NUMBER FIFTEEN: REBELLION

2 Samuel 15:10-12 (KJV) But Absalom sent spies throughout all the tribes of Israel, saying, as soon as ye hear the sound of the trumpet, then ye shall say, Absalom reigneth in Hebron. {11} And with Absalom went two hundred men out of Jerusalem, that were called; and they went in their simplicity, and they knew not any thing. And the conspiracy was strong; for the people increased continually with Absalom.

Absalom ends up leading a rebellion and runs David out of Jerusalem. David and his men flee to the hills. Absalom comes in and takes over Jerusalem.

NUMBER SIXTEEN: ADULTERY AND FORNICATION

As I said, Absalom came into the city; David left ten of his concubines. This is really fulfillment of scripture that says, "You will have evil in your house." Nathan told David what he did in secret God would repay him openly. Absalom came into Jerusalem and took all ten of David's concubines. We struggled; I talked with my Pastor about this. How you list a concubine that is not legally, lawfully, a wife but I really do believe adultery and fornication come under this curse.

NUMBER SEVENTEEN: ACCIDENTS

2 Samuel 18:9 (KJV) And Absalom rode upon a mule, and the mule went under the thick boughs of a great oak, and his head caught hold of the oak, and he was taken up between the heaven and the earth; and the mule that was under him went away.

When Absalom's rebellion is nearly over, Absalom goes riding off on his donkey. He goes riding through some oaks. He was known for his long beautiful hair and this long beautiful hair got caught up in the branches and literally picked him up off his donkey. And he hung there between heaven and earth. The Word says, Joab, David's chief officer, came along and found him. He ran a spear through his heart and killed him.

NUMBER EIGHTTEEN: IDOLATRY

2 Samuel 18:18 (KJV) Now Absalom in his lifetime had taken and reared up for himself a pillar, which is in the king's dale: for he said, I have no son to keep my name in remembrance: and he called the pillar after his own name: and it is called unto this day, Absalom's place.

We will go into idolatry more when we get down to Solomon.

NUMBER NINETEEN: FALSE COMPASSION

2 Samuel 18:33-19:6 (KJV) and the king was much moved, and went up to the chamber over the gate, and wept: and as he went, thus he said, O my son Absalom, my son, my son Absalom! Would God I had died for thee, O Absalom, my son, my son! {19:1} and it was told Joab, Behold, the king weepeth and mourneth for Absalom. {2} and the victory that day was turned into mourning unto all the people: for the people heard say that day how the king was grieved for his son. {3} And the people gat them by stealth that day into the city, as people being ashamed steal away when they flee in battle. {4} But the king covered his face, and the king cried with a loud voice, O my son Absalom, O Absalom, my son, my son! {5} And Joab came into the house to the king, and said, Thou hast shamed this day the faces of all thy servants, which this day have saved thy life, and the lives of thy sons and of thy daughters, and the lives of thy wives, and the lives of thy concubines; {6} In that thou lovest thine enemies, and hatest thy friends. For thou hast declared this day, that thou regardest neither princes nor servants: for this day I perceive, that if Absalom had lived, and all we had died this day, then it had pleased thee well.

I want to say it is an unbalanced compassion. When Absalom dies and David is told, he falls apart. He throws himself on the ground, rips his clothes, throws dust over himself and mourns. This is the same man who has just tried to kill him, who has killed his son, who has led armed revolt. Here, David is just totally distraught over what has happened. It is a false compassion. There should have been compassion because Absalom did wrong. There should always be compassion for that. David went overboard in his response to his death.

NUMBER TWENTY: STRIVING AND STRIFE

2 Samuel 22:44 (KJV) Thou also hast delivered me from the strivings of my people, thou hast kept me to be head of the heathen: a people which I knew not shall serve me.

One of the many things in my life was strife before God set me free. My life often caused strife with other people and whenever I was in a situation involving strife. I would respond often out of anger.

NUMBER TWENTY-ONE: THE VIOLENT MAN

2 Samuel 22:49 (KJV) and that bringeth me forth from mine enemies: thou also hast lifted me up on high above them that rose up against me: thou hast delivered me from the violent man.

The literal translation says, "God delivered me from the violent man." Every commentator I read on that verse infers that "the violent man" is Saul. But in part, I think David also had Absalom on his heart, here. I cannot help thinking about that when I read about David's heart attitude towards what happened to his son.

I know, one of the seven demonic personalities I was delivered of was specifically called the "violent man." I think that is something we find under this curse, a violent man.

NUMBER TWENTY-TWO: SEXUAL LUSTS, LUST THAT LEADS TO IDOLATRY

1 Kings 11:1-11 (KJV) But king Solomon loved many strange women, together with the daughter of Pharaoh, women of the Moabites, Ammonites, Edomites, Zidonians, and Hittites; {2} Of the nations concerning which the LORD said unto the children of Israel, Ye shall not go in to them, neither shall they come in unto you: for surely they will turn away your heart after their gods: Solomon clave unto these in love. {3} and he had seven hundred wives, princesses, and three hundred concubines: and his wives turned away his heart. {4} for it came to pass, when Solomon was old, that his wives turned away his heart after other gods: and his heart was not perfect with the LORD his God, as was the heart of David his father. {5} for Solomon went after Ashtoreth the goddess of the Zidonians, and after Milcom the abomination of the Ammonites. {6} And Solomon did evil in the sight of the LORD, and went not fully after the LORD, as did David his father. {7} Then did Solomon build a high place for Chemosh, the abomination of Moab, in the hill that is before Jerusalem, and for Molech, the abomination of the children of Ammon. {8}

And likewise did he for all his strange wives, which burnt incense and sacrificed unto their gods. {9} And the LORD was angry with Solomon, because his heart was turned from the LORD God of Israel, which had appeared unto him twice, {10} And had commanded him concerning this thing, that he should not go after other gods: but he kept not that which the LORD commanded. {11} Wherefore the LORD said unto Solomon, Forasmuch as this is done of thee, and thou hast not kept my covenant and my statutes, which I have commanded thee, I will surely rend the kingdom from thee, and will give it to thy servant.

Here it talks about Solomon's falling away from God. It differs from physical lust in this way, if you look at all the cults; many of them use perverted sex to attract new converts. Jesus called us to be fishers of men, but they have a term they like to use, called, "flirty fishing" they use sex, pornographic videos. They use all sorts of different methods to attract predominately young people, to get them. They believe in marriage but live a communal lifestyle. They openly practice wife swapping. Sex is the big center point of the cult. I think that is one of the things we need to be aware of, that the enemy can use this type of lust to bring us into idolatry.

I just want to make a comment about Solomon because there was no evidence of the curse in his early life. Solomon was a godly king when he started out. There is no doubt about it. He had a heart after God. He had tremendous wisdom, tremendous knowledge, but there was no evidence of the curse in his life. It did not show up until later. I think it is the same, today, in us. Just because there's no evidence of these traits in our life does not mean we are not under the curse. It means for some reason they have not shown up yet, or they may show up later.

It is something you cannot say, "Because it is not there today I do not have it." It could very well be there dormant, and you may not even know it. I did not know it. I just knew something was wrong. We have to understand that it could show up at any time. You have to have a word from the Lord to say, "Yes, that is something that controls you. That it is over you."

NUMBER TWENTY-THREE: ADVERSARIES

1 Kings 11:25 (KJV) and he was an adversary to Israel all the days of Solomon, beside the mischief that Hadad did: and he abhorred Israel, and reigned over Syria.

We see in Solomon's life once he falls into idolatry that he gets all sorts of adversaries coming against him. For the first time in his ruler-ship Israel came under tremendous outside pressure. As his name implied, Israel lived a peaceful existence up until this time. Then, suddenly everybody in the world starts coming against the nation of Israel.

CHAPTER 5

The Curse Follows David's Line

Let's look at ten generations following David. What happened with the Kings, what happened to his offspring? I'm not going to fully cover all of them because of time. You need to see that it doesn't stop with just David's children, it continues.

We looked at Solomon, who was the first generation after David, the first king following David. The next king following Solomon was Rehoboam. He was the first king of Judah. It was under his reign that the nation of Judah and Israel split because of his own sin. Rehoboam literally means "The enlarger of the people."

It's kind of interesting that the nation was separated under his reign. Rehoboam lacked wisdom. The kingdom was divided because of his cruelty. He tried to reunite the kingdom by force. His mother was an Amonitess. He worshiped God but was tolerant of heathen worship and immorality. The last one he gave up was temple treasure for the peace of the nation. He gave up all the treasures of the temple Solomon had made. The key verse concerning Rehoboam is 2 Chronicles 12:14 (KJV):

And he did evil, because he prepared not his heart to seek the LORD.

"God, how many times have I not prepared my heart to seek You? How many times as a result of that, have I done evil in Your sight? I hate to count it but I am sure one day I will hear that. We have a good friend, Eleanor. She likes to say that at the Bema Seat judgement we will all stand there and it will be like being at a drive-in. There will be a huge theater; because it is eternity, and there is no time we see each one's life played out on this screen. For me this concept is kind of devastating. You will know me for exactly who I am. You will have seen everything in my life. In part that makes me want to live a transparent life here so you are not surprised when you see all the mean and nasty things I have done, all the times my heart has not been prepared to seek God.

The next king was called, Abia. The literal translation is "Whose father is God." Abia walked in all the sins of his father, Rehoboam. You also see he knew the covenant he lived under. Not a lot is said about Abia. He only reigned three years.

The third king following Solomon was Asa. He was the first good king, the first one classified as being a good king. Asa's name means "healing, or to heal." Asa did what was good and right in the eyes of the Lord. He trusted God when one million Ethiopians attacked him. He also used temple treasures to buy help from Syria, rather than trust

God. He followed prophetic words when the prophetic word was pleasant. When the prophetic wasn't pleasant he killed the prophet. He oppressed the people. His reign started out good. He reigned forty-one years. In the end, he ended up trusting physicians instead of God. Remember his name means healing, or to be healed. He died from a disease in his feet. Nice guy? He didn't live up to his name very well, either.

The next king is Jehoshaphat. The name means "Jehovah Judged." He's the first good king in Judah. He was a zealous follower of God. He seems to have made only one mistake in his whole reign. He trusted in an alliance with Ahab, at one point. From then on, he trusted God when attacked by his enemies. I think the name "Jehovah Judged," is very significant. We should be a people who would say, "Jehovah Judged, we can be zealous followers of God." We could be classified as good stewards. We could be classified as faithful.

The next king was Joram that means, "Jehovah is high." He had a nice relationship with God. He knew God was up there someplace high. Joram married the daughter of Ahab who was the worst king Israel ever knew. He walked in the ways of the kings of Israel rather than the kings of Judah. He did evil in the sight of the Lord. He introduced idolatry and established Baal worship. He caused the people of Judah to commit fornication. He killed all of his brothers so that none of them could take his place, except for one God managed to save. He died of an incurable stomach disease. He was such a bad king he was not even buried in the tombs of the Kings. The nation would not even acknowledge him.

Ahaziah, "Held by Jehovah," was the son-in-law of Ahab. He did evil in the sight of the Lord by walking in the way of Ahab. He had an alliance with Israel against Syria. Jehu killed him. Jehu was a soldier anointed by Elisha. He was commissioned to kill the house of Ahab. He killed all the descendants of Ahaziah and Ahab's daughter.

The next king is Joash whose name means "Jehovah has given." He was the third good king. He did what was right in the sight of the Lord during the life of his uncle, Jehoiada, the priest. When his uncle the priest dies he fell into idolatry. He kills the prophet who rebuked him for his idolatry. He bought peace with Syria with the treasures of the house of the Lord. This is a story that is repeated over and over and over again. I wonder how many times it is that we try to buy peace in our life by giving up some of the treasures of God, in our own life?

I have seen times where I have tried to do it rather than simply trusting God to win the war for us. We try to make our own peace or find our own way of doing it. He was plagued with a great disease. He was not even lucky enough to die from the plague. His servants finally killed him. He just suffered for a few years.

The next king is Amaziah whose name means, "Whom Jehovah strengthens." He did right in the sight of the Lord, not quite like David, he followed the law. He hired warriors from Israel and was rebuked for hiring them. He responded properly to the prophetic Word. He was obedient to God. He gained victory over Edom because he trusted God, then he brings home the gods of Edom to worship. He let Israel take gold and silver from the house of God. Finally, he's murdered.

The last one is Uzziah whose name means, "Jehovah is strength." He did what was right in the sight of the Lord. God prospered him as long as he sought Him. II Chronicles 26:16 is the key verse in Uzziah's life.

2 Chronicles 26:16 (KJV) But when he was strong, his heart was lifted up to his destruction: for he transgressed against the LORD his God, and went into the temple of the LORD to burn incense upon the altar of incense.

He decides he's going to take over the rule of the priests. Uzziah goes into the temple to offer incense and because he did that, the Lord smote him with leprosy, and he finally died a leper. I have a couple of interesting thoughts. It seems to me all of Israel's problems stem from the sin of one man. I kind of wonder what would have happened to the nation of Israel if David would not have taken Bathsheba and killed Urriah the Hittite. I wonder whether things might have been different, but because of that, and the problems that were brought into his family, the nation ended up being divided. The nation rebelled and the nation eventually falls into captivity and taken to Babylon.

We see the same thing in Adam that it only took one sin for Adam to fall. I wonder in my own life could it be just one more sin where God said, enough is enough." That gives me a tremendous fear of God; it gives me a tremendous respect. I am not plagued by it, but it causes me to help control my steps. It causes me to think about what I am doing before I do it.

I found one interesting coincidence through the whole thing. When David falls into sin with Bathsheba and introduces the curse of the bastard into his own home, David and Israel have just come from a great victory over the children of Ammon. These people were a cursed people because they were under the curse of the Bastard. I wonder how many times we figure we have gained victory over a sin to find we have fallen into it. We win a great victory over this sin, and suddenly there is another, smack in our face again. It is in verse one, that David gained victory, and in verse two, David's up on the roof, and there is Bathsheba. I find that kind of interesting.

> *2 Samuel 11:1-3 (KJV) And it came to pass, after the year was expired, at the time when kings go forth to battle, that David sent Joab, and his servants with him, and all Israel; and they destroyed the children of Ammon, and besieged Rabbah. But David tarried still at Jerusalem. {2} And it came to pass in an eveningtide, that David arose from off his bed, and walked upon the roof of the king's house: and from the roof he saw a woman washing herself; and the woman was very beautiful to look upon. {3} And David sent and inquired after the woman. And one said, Is not this Bathsheba, the daughter of Eliam, the wife of Uriah the Hittite?*

David worshipped God through the Psalms. When you look at David's offspring, however, none of them were worshippers, with the exception of Solomon, for a brief period of time. That is peculiar in a nation whose national life is centered on the worship of God: how their kings could not be worshippers in general. There are two references in all the story of David and his offspring; there are two references about David's children being involved with God. One says of Absalom, "He made a vow to the God of heaven," and there is no example that he paid attention to the vow. It is kind of like going into court and putting your hand on the Bible and swearing in the name of God to tell the truth the whole truth and nothing but the truth, but not caring a bit about the Word of God.

The other one is Adonijah, who was I believe David's third son. He should have been the legitimate heir to the throne after Absalom died. When David proclaimed Solomon to be king, Adonijah fled into the temple and grabbed the horns which were on the altar, which were there for a place of refuge. This is the man who tried to forcibly take the kingdom from David, before David dies. There again is nothing in the Word that this man had a relationship with God. He hoped God would protect him. He ran to the protection of God without knowing God. And those are the only two, particularly of David's children, the only two examples of any of them ever worshipping God. Some of the other kings worshiped God, some for a period, some not at all. It is funny that a nation whose central purpose was to worship God was so completely disobedient to that.

CHAPTER 6

The Source of Freedom from Curses

II Peter 1-11 (KJV). *Simon Peter, a servant and an apostle of Jesus Christ, to them that have obtained like precious faith with us through the righteousness of God and our Savior, Jesus Christ: Grace and peace be multiplied unto you through the knowledge of God, and of Jesus, our Lord, according as his divine power hath given unto us all things that pertain unto life and godliness, through the knowledge of him that hath called us to glory and virtue; by which are given unto us exceedingly great and precious promises, that by these ye might be partakers of the divine nature, having escaped the corruption that is in the world through lust. And beside this, giving all diligence, add to your faith virtue; and to virtue, knowledge; and to knowledge, self-control; and to self-control, patience; and to patience, godliness; and to godliness, brotherly kindness; and to brotherly kindness, love. For if these things be in you, and abound, they make you that ye shall neither be barren nor unfruitful in the knowledge of our Lord Jesus Christ. but he that lacketh these things is blind and cannot see afar off, and hath forgotten that he was purged from his old sins. Wherefore the rather, brethren, give diligence to make your calling and election sure; for if ye do these things, ye shall never fall. For so an entrance shall be ministered unto you abundantly into the everlasting kingdom of our Lord and Savior, Jesus Christ.*

I have meditated on Verse Ten for probably six years now. I

keep digging out the little piece of paper I copied it on and stuck it on my bed. I looked at it every night. "Wherefore rather brethren give diligence to make your calling and election sure for if you do these things you shall never fall."

What I have been trying to share with you in the last few pages are the culmination of seeking to understand this verse, the giving diligence to make your calling and election sure.

One of the things we sometimes look at concerning God's deliverance is the liberty it brings us. The liberty is wonderful; there is no doubt about that. While we were worshipping the morning I taught this, the Lord said to me, "Liberty without restraint leads to lawlessness." We cannot just look at the liberty God is going to bring us into, and has already brought us into, and just be glad and rejoice in that liberty. If we concentrate on just the liberty, we are going to end up missing the mark again. What God would like for us to do, is take the liberty He has brought us into, and use it to bring about the sureness of the calling, the calling that is a part of each of our lives. The restraint will help keep us in order. If we will do that, we can take the liberty and the restraint and it will produce something not only in our own life, but we will be able to minister to other people.

We do not all share the same gifting or the same calling. The body cannot use fifteen hearts; it can only use one heart. It cannot use five feet; it only uses two. We all have special functions and purposes here. In this last move of God, He wants His Body to walk in the callings and purposes that He has given to the Church. That is what the world wants to see. If we do that we walk as a united Body. If we walk as a whole Body the world will go WOW!!

The reason the church, particularly the church behind the iron curtain, is so effective in their witness, is because the people walk in the purposes of God. They know there is no hope other than what can be found in Jesus. They know there is nothing else. The government offers nothing to these people. Because of this, and what they see in the body, it means something to them. The church is growing phenomenally in China, Russia and other parts of the world.

I would like to share some of the Word and a little more of my own experience. We've been talking about the curse of the bastard found in Deuteronomy 23:2 (KJV):

A bastard shall not enter into the congregation of the LORD; even to his tenth generation shall he not enter into the congregation of the LORD.

Basically, the curse of the bastard separates us from God and from the people of God. It hinders us in our walk of becoming who and what we are supposed to be in the Lord.

I would like to share two things that the enemy brought to me to try to convince me that this curse was not true.

We looked predominately at David and his family. When I began to think and meditate about David's family, the first thing that came to me was Psalm 51. That has always been a very favorite Scripture of mine, and I understand now why. Psalm 51 talks about how David repented for his sin with Bathsheba and killing Urriah. I said, "God, why did David's prayer of repentance not break the curse in David's life?" That is what the enemy was trying to convince me, that it wasn't true and was trying to introduce doubt and unbelief. So, I began to say, "God, why, was it that David's repentance did not do anything about breaking the curse?"

What God immediately told me was, "In David's case there was no blood. They had a blood sacrifice but it was of an animal. David could receive forgiveness for himself, but the only way to break a curse was through the blood sacrifice of Jesus." That is the only way it can be done. There was no provision made at that point in history for breaking curses other than that blood sacrifice of Jesus. So, while David could receive forgiveness for his own sin, he could not do anything for the iniquities he had committed.

I wish I could tell you that I understand everything about sin, iniquity, and transgression, but I do not. I've gone back to notes we received in Bible College in England on sin, iniquity and transgression and have studied more since. I still do not understand it in its entirety. There is a difference between sin, iniquity and transgression. In the Word, there is clear distinction. While I have always looked at these words as sin, labeled everything as sin, to God there is a difference.

One of the teachings talked about the fact that sin is what I do myself; it is the iniquity that I pass onto my generations. That is what it says in the Ten Commandments. It says the iniquity of the father is passed onto the third and fourth generation. It does not say the sin. It distinguishes it, and says it is the iniquities that are passed on.

When you look at Psalm 103, it says He forgives their iniquities and heals all their diseases. It does not say sin it says their iniquities. In Isaiah 53, again, it talks about the iniquities. When it talks about Jesus' sacrifice it talks about how He was bruised for our iniquities. It is not sin; it's our iniquities. So, I finally said, "Okay Lord, I understand that, I think, I will believe your Word and put trust in it."

When I taught this the first time, I shared for three weeks about the curse of the Bastard. I shared the first week predominantly of my testimony up until October 1987. I shared some of the experiences of my life, the hurts, and the pain and how angry and bitter I was.

The next week I shared from the Word of God what it says concerning the curse of the bastard. The truth about how this curse affected me needs to be understood through my life today.

When it comes down to the bottom line the reality of my changed life speaks of what God has done in my life; that is the reality of what I've experienced out of this. It's been tremendous. It's not just a little, but God has done it all. He has set me free from a life of misery, for my wife, my family, and me. He has given us all a new life.

If I sat and shared everything that God has done, that I know God has done since October 1988, it would take another volume. I don't have time to do that. The biggest thing God's has done in my life is that He has broken the power of guilt and sin when He set me free from this curse. The teaching of Romans Chapters Six and Seven, says that there is a spiritual power. It is called the law of sin and death. I read it and read it.

I know theologians throughout the years have read it and read it. It took Luther to finally get some understanding of what this was all about. There is actually a spiritual force called sin, and it affects believers' lives. One of the out-workings of this power, this spiritual force, is guilt and condemnation. That used to tear me up. There is no other way to put it. It used to destroy my life. Every time I would start walking in the things of the Lord, try to get anywhere close to doing what God had called me to do, along came this power and ripped the legs right out from underneath me, and I would do something stupid! I would get in a fight; it just went on and on. Since this thing has been broken, it is not there. It is not to say I do not sin anymore. I am still human. I still live in a body of flesh with fleshly desires. There is no longer the pull, the pull, the pull to do that, which is ungodly. That is, what I know I should not do, I do. I do not know how else to explain it. There is no longer any condemnation. I still make mistakes. I still do things at home that I should not do. However, the enemy has had no foothold to come into my life now and make me guilty. That in and of itself is tremendous freedom!

Exodus 20:20 is a verse that has become very real to us.

Exodus 20:20 (KJV) *and Moses said unto the people, Fear not: for God is come to prove you, and that his fear may be before your faces, that ye sin not.*

That has become such a reality to us. There were things, Libbie and I have wanted to do for a long, long time and it was not wrong, it was not even sin. However, the appearance of it probably was not in line with what we should do. Suddenly, in December, we had a chance to do this, and immediately, we found we could not do it, because of the fear.

The fear of the Lord is something I struggled over for years; I didn't really understand what it meant. I was getting on U.S. 10, onto I-75, about four years ago. I slipped in between two semi-trucks, right on the bumper of one, and the front bumper of the other was right behind me. God said, "That's the fear of the Lord." I said, "Huh?" He said, "It understands that the power to destroy you is there, but when the power is used within the limits of the law, there is safety. The power will not destroy you." I went, "Oh yeah."

Then suddenly, I realized God's law for me is His grace and His mercy. As long as I do not violate Him, do not violate His law, I live. But if He wanted to, and I violated His purposes, He could wipe me out. It has brought tremendous deliverance. It has changed the way I do things, now.

Romans 8:1-17, talks about adoption. God wants to adopt us as His children. He has done it spiritually, but He wants us to draw so close to the heart of the Father, it is unbelievable! We vaguely comprehend how close God wants us to live in Him because He is the Father of Fathers. The Father of the fatherless, from the beginning of the Word to the end of the Word, the one theme that comes out more than any other is God cares for widows. He cares for the orphan. It is the Father's heart to care for orphans. He loves orphans and we were all orphans until we said, "Lord, I believe you."

The other thing this has done for me is healed me from rejection. I used to have great difficulty standing in a room of people because of the feelings of rejection. I have looked back, I look back all the time, and there is no longer any rejection. It does not motivate my life anymore. It does not cause me to do stupid things like it used to.

One of the other things I would like to point out is that being released from the curse of the Bastard is not a cure all for the flesh. While God in setting me free from this curse, which has brought many changes in my flesh, I still struggle with that which is the biggest struggle, my weight. God is dealing with me to change that, to discipline that area of my life. But I still struggle with the flesh. Getting set free from a curse is not going to cause you to crucify the flesh. That is something that comes through a whole different procedure. That is something we have to take the responsibility of our self.

Some of the other things God has set me free from are fantasy and double-mindedness. I used to live in a real fantasy world in different areas of my life. That is no longer a part of my life. I understand things in the reality of the situation and the circumstance.

DEPRESSION. All my life I have struggled with depression. I have had doctors tell me, "Well, it is not clinical depression. It is not this, or it is not that." At its worst, it used to lock me away for a week at a time, or longer, I could not face anybody. I could not face anything. Call it what you want, but that has continued in some form up until October 1988. Situations would come, and depression would try to destroy me. That is no longer there. Depression does still come around at times to try to and do me in. It's not situations or circumstances we find ourselves in that bring us down, but we will share a little later what happens when that comes around. When that happens, I start thinking about the Lord, and you cannot do that for very long and remain in a depressed state.

DOUBT AND UNBELIEF, ANGER, REBELLIOUS SPIRIT. My rebellion predominantly had to do with fighting against God's plans and purposes for my life. I am not saying it was limited to that but suddenly, I have accepted God's plan's and purposes in my life, and the walk is no longer a struggle. It is just an acceptance, a submission to the will of God.

SPIRITUAL BLINDNESS AND DEAFNESS. Prior to being set free from this curse I could not see or hear spiritual things. Afterwards, the gifts of discernment of spirits and sensing God through dreams and visions were much more vivid in my life.

INSANITY. The one thing I thought about the most was insanity. I have had to deal with this all throughout my life. Every time God would bring deliverance (for the first eight years of my Christian walk), I just knew this was it. There was not going to be anymore, but somehow, I was always plagued with the fear that I would go through those emotions. I thought this as I wrote and realized for almost three years I have not had that feeling! I know this thing is over with. There are some conditions I have to live under, now, but it is not going to come back. God has broken this thing once and for all.

SEXUAL IMMORALITY. Because of the mind-games and the fantasy I had a lot of problems with fantasy lust. That is gone. Due to the personal nature of it, I cannot share that much. There are things God has done in my life in the last three years that have changed the way I deal sexually with everything. I never was one who went out and ran around. I just did not do that. Most of it was in the mind. That is gone. What you conceive in the mind first, sooner or later gets to the body. I knew that if I continued to do that sooner or later the enemy would set up something and get me involved in other ways.

TORMENTING SPIRITS, HOPELESSNESS AND SUICIDE. They are gone, they are gone, and they are gone! Hallelujah! Unless you have dealt with severe mental torment you cannot comprehend what it is like. I have never experienced a lot of physical problems; maybe some of the physical problems are similar, but I know mental torment. I listened to a thing on the radio where they brought a bunch of handicapped people into a school to let the children learn to relate to handicapped people. They were "physical handicapped" this and that. They never mentioned one who was mentally handicapped in anyway.

Mental handicaps will destroy your life. We heard a story about a man who had weighed 1200 pounds. He lost 400 pounds and he is now down to about 800 pounds. That is a mental torment that drives an individual to weigh 1200 pounds. He had not been out of his bedroom for seventeen years. Now that he has lost 400 pounds he managed to get to the living room the other day. He could not force himself to leave the house. Mental torment like that destroys an individual's life. To be free of that... I cannot explain it unless you've been there.

Those are things God has freed me from. The things I have experiencing are, first, joy. I need to say something about joy. I am not of the nature and personalities to go flittering around, real bubbly and outgoing. That is not who I am. That is not the spiritual force of joy. That is fine if that is your personality and make-up. That is wonderful! To me in the five months of walking this out, from the time I was set free until the time I taught it for the first time; I see joy in my life. Not just the bubbly, giggly feelings. It has become an inner strength that continues on in all situations with peace and contentment, knowing God has all things in His control.

> **James 1:2** (KJV) *"Brethren, count it all joy when you fall into diverse temptations."*

I do not care what we need to go through, we go through it joyfully knowing that God, in God's capacity as God, has it all under control and is the reality of Romans 8:35-39 which says:

> **Romans 8:35-39 (KJV)** *who shall separate us from the love of Christ? Shall tribulation, or distress, or persecution, or famine, or nakedness, or peril, or sword? {36} as it is written, for thy sake we are killed all the day long; we are accounted as sheep for the slaughter. {37} Nay, in all these things we are more than conquerors through him that loved us. {38} for I am persuaded, that neither death, nor life, nor angels, nor principalities, nor powers, nor things present, nor things to come, {39} nor height, nor depth, nor any other creature, shall be able to separate us from the love of God, which is in Christ Jesus our Lord.*

There is nothing that will separate us from the love of God! There is not a demon in hell that can separate us from the love of God! Beloved, you need to know that, because of what is about to happen with the releasing of God's spirit in a new way. There is going to be a release from hell of hordes of demons like we've never seen before.

You need to know there is nothing, nothing in the world, physical or spiritual, that can separate you from the love of God! That is what will get us through! That is what will bring revival in our own life! That is what will turn the world upside down-by knowing that God's love is inseparable from us. We've come into peace. Again, it goes back to being released from mental torment.

GOD'S PRESENCE. Suddenly, I was walking in God's presence. It's an interesting word study to go through a Concordance and look at what God's presence does in our lives. The first thing God told me (after I was freed from this), was in His presence is fullness of joy. I thought, "WOW!!!" I have experienced the presence of the Lord from time to time, but because of the sin, because of the guilt, I keep trying to separate myself from God. When we were in England I came to the understanding that when I sinned I used to run <u>from</u> the cross. God wants us to run <u>to</u> the cross; He does not want us to run from Him because we have sinned. That is the time we need to run closer, to get closer to Him. It is His presence that will sustain us.

Go through your Concordance. It is just outstanding! Our enemies fall, and perish in God's presence! Justice comes in God's presence. We are hidden from the pride of man and strife, in God's presence. The presence of God will cause us to know the fear of the Lord. We will know that times of refreshing come from the presence of the Lord.

I have come into a greater understanding and greater exercise of the gift of discernment of spirits. That used to cause me a lot of problems when I would start battling with a spirit, either openly in the heavenlies, or working with another individual. I now understand what is going on so that I do not wrestle with the individual. I wrestle with the power and principality behind the situation, not the individual. If you cannot do anything with that, leave the situation alone. Do not try to fight it. I used to fight the individual. It does not work that way.

CLARITY IN HEARING WHEN GOD SPEAKS. I have always heard God speak. I have always been very open to Him. I will use the word "voices," but again, it is not a literal voice, not an audible voice. Mom used to keep telling me all the time, "You need to be careful of which voice is speaking to you." She was right. A lot of times I used to listen to the wrong voices. I have heard God speak in the last few months. I heard God speak about the things He wants us to do. He has brought us to an open door. God has given us something to do. We covet your prayers. If we are going to do the thing God has shown us to do it is going to take a lot of prayer.

CONTENTMENT. I am content where we are. There are probably not many people who could walk where God has called Libbie and I to walk and that is okay, because we could not walk where God has called you to walk, either. I fought God. "God, I do not want to do this, I do not want to live like this." Suddenly, we are content. We know that God is going to take care of everything. There is not a lot of strain; there is not a lot of fighting. You just sit back and say, "We will see what God is going to do." God has never let us down.

I shared on provision just before we went to South Carolina. The stories I could tell you about since that time on how we watched God provide! We should have lost our car, the Renault. We have never had the liberty to share this before. We made one payment in fourteen months, because there was no money. There just was no money to make a car payment. We got back up, and talked to the credit union. I occasionally would call them and say, "Hey, what is going on?"

For the first five months, I called and said we are a little behind in our car payment, and they pulled up their computer and said, "Oh no, we show you do not owe for another month." I had not made a payment in five months, "You must have made more payments." No. "You must have paid more each month than what you paid." "No, we did not." So, we got through that. January came and we were able to make a payment in January. That was the last one until October. We talked to these people. God told us how to deal with them, to deal honestly with them.

I spent a couple of days, a couple of appointments with the assistant manager of the credit union. I told him this is the way it is going to be because that is the way God told us it was going to be. If you do not like it, that is all we can do. Here are the keys to the car. It meant nothing to me any longer. He said, "What do you have?" I said we have a Seventy Dodge. It works very well. It does not look very good but it gets us where we want to go. So, they kept our car for a week. We kept praying.

Before that happened, we had decided that's what we were going to do, that we weren't going to live under their pressure. We decided to give the tires to a friend when he was getting the pastor's car. We had about 5,000 miles on the top-of-the-line Michelin's. It caused some people some difficulty but I knew what God had said, so we gave them away.

Suddenly, we get the car back. They accepted the terms God had said to offer them. God worked it out God took care of us. We got new tires, we got C.V. joints, we got a brake job, we got shocks, struts and we paid about a third of what it would have cost to actually have that work done, going to a garage! God worked out the circumstances.

I went for a brake job and was told, "We cannot get you in today. Can we do it tomorrow?" I said, "Fine." He said, "You are from Midland. Why not take it to our Midland store?" I said, "Fine." As soon as I said that, the Spirit of the Lord said, "He is not going to want to do that job for the price they have in the paper."

I walked in the next morning, and sure enough. He did not want to do that job. The enemy had set me up. My old nature two months before would have blown up at this guy and said, "Hey! This is what you told us you were going to do. You're going to do this for ninety bucks." They found every excuse. They pulled off the tire, they found we had a bad C.V. joint, and He said that's another $300.00, blah, blah, blah. He kept building the thing up. So, I said "Fine, put the tires on. I will go home."

The next day I got a ninety-dollar brake job for thirty dollars! That is God! That is how God works. And the C.V. joints which he said would cost three to four hundred dollars to repair, while I was driving home God said, "Go look at your extended warranty." Sure enough C.V. joints are covered under our extended warranty. It cost $17.32. That is God! It's been marvelous!

Since that time in the winter of 1988, God has increased our income almost 700 percent. I now see how God has set us free from a curse of poverty by being freed from this curse. We still keep in perspective what Paul wrote the Philippians:

Philippians 4:12 (KJV) I know both how to be abased, and I know how to abound: everywhere and in all things, I am instructed both to be full and to be hungry, both to abound and to suffer need.

STABILITY. I have never known the stability as we have experienced it these last years.

FINDING SATISFACTION IN MY ROLE AS A FATHER. There is nothing greater to me right now; Fatherhood has always been a responsibility and all sorts of other things. My children are now very precious. I enjoy it when my son will allow me to rock him to sleep at night. It is not very often, but we are working on that.

DEVELOPING A GREATER UNDERSTANDING OF WHO I AM IN CHRIST. Understand, I do not have all the nagging doubts about myself, anymore; I know what God has done for me.

RECEIVING A RELEASE IN MY PRAYER LIFE. If you have ever struggled with praying in tongues... God has changed my prayer life completely around since being released. I used to struggle to pray fifteen minutes a week. As I taught this I was praying an hour or two a morning in the Spirit. It is no longer a bother. I look forward to it.

I got done with the second hour and I thought, "God, I want to do this some more."

I HAVE BEEN RELEASED TO SEEK GOD. My mind has been freed to work properly, through the Word, through the prayer. Suddenly, I have come into a relationship with the Father that I have never experienced before, never known. When I got the letter stating who my biological parents were, it said the "<u>alleged father</u>." That has been part of the problem. With my adoptive parents, my dad went through some tremendous struggles and I was never real close to him. We did a lot of things when I was quite young, but his work, plus his drinking problem, separated us quite often. I never knew a father; immediately here is a Father relationship! "I have never known this before, God, you are my Father. You really are MY Father! Here's Father!" You hear God speaking, to you. You feel the Father's heart. Often, I feel the Father's heart; I feel how grieved the Father is. How He loves us. How He wants to love us freely and openly. I weep, I cry. And it's not that I don't have joy, but God wants to love us in ways we resist.

<u>CHAPTER 7</u>

Staying Free of the Power of Curses

God has showed me some ways to break free from the curse. It is not something you can say, "Okay we are going to break the power of it, and that's it. We will never have any problems with it again." I know that there are some things that God did. There are things God has given me to do to help me maintain freedom. The first one is thankfulness. I am so very thankful, day in and day out, moment by moment of who God is in my life, in my family's life, in the life of our church. I just keep expressing that to Him. A lot of times I use music and tell Him through song, "God, I'm thankful, I'm thankful." See Philippians 4:6-8. Be thankful!

The second thing that's probably been the most important to me, I shared when I had problems with depression, and how I would spend time and meditate on the depression. Well God showed me to take the times that I meditated on the depression and the self-pity, and meditate on Him. When things get a little rough, if I just take a couple of minutes and meditate on just God, just the things I am thankful for, often, that is enough to stop it. If certain situations are bad, and circumstances get rough, the thing He has brought home to me is the reality of the Lamb of

God.

In John 1:29, when Jesus comes to be baptized John the Baptist turns and says:

John 1:29 (KJV), *The next day John seeth Jesus coming unto him, and saith, behold the Lamb of God, which taketh away the sin of the world.*

For five months, I've been meditating almost daily, on this verse. Jesus truly was to be the Lamb of God. The sacrifice that God Himself made, God the Father: because He loved us, He gave us Jesus.

I have learned something in meditating. We saw a movie at Christmas on the life of Jesus, on our local Christian television station. It was very good, but when it got to the crucifixion, something bothered me about it. Here is this man on the cross in what I will call a pristine condition, a little blood because of the crown of thorns, but I realized something. Our art, our paintings, and our movies have robbed us of something of the reality of what Calvary truly cost God. Jesus when He went to the cross, not only bore our sins, but He was broken in body. I do not mean broken bones. If I can get one thing across to you this would be what I'd like you to understand. When they arrested Jesus, they took Him to the high priest, and while He was there He was under the guard of the temple solders (guards). They were not Romans. They were Jews. They consisted of approximately 600 men and for the night these 600 men beat Jesus. That is what the Word says. They beat Him with their fists; they beat Him about the head and face, continuously, until His face was a bloody mess. It said they blindfolded Him, and when it says blindfolded, they wrapped a covering over His head so as to blindfold Him. The purpose, they said was not to identify who struck Him. They were mocking Him. Not only were they beating Him, they were mocking Him.

In Isaiah 52:14 it says:

Isaiah 52:14 (KJV) *as many were astonied at thee; his visage was so marred more than any man and his form more than the sons of men:*

Scofield has a footnote on that; it says, "The literal rending is terrible. He was so marred from the form of man that His aspect and His appearance was not that of the Son of Man;" not human. The beating was so fierce that His face did not have the form of a human face. <u>God, You loved us that much that You would do that for me.</u>

I have worked in a hospital; I have seen many bad accident cases come into the intensive care units. I have seen massive skull injuries, and I think God, what <u>You, Jesus</u> experienced was so much worse than anything I have seen there. I cannot understand love like that.

After the temple guards finished beating Him, they took Him to the Romans. The Romans scourged Him. They took a whip, and the whip was made of leather, twelve leather straps, and in the leather straps were bound bits of bone and bits of metal. They hit Him thirty-nine times with that leather whip. Most men died under that kind of punishment. They opened up His entire back from His head to the bottom of His heels. Thy opened His back with wounds so that it was one wound. This is what it cost Jesus to get us a relationship with Him, a relationship with the Father. You go on; the crucifixion was a horrible manner of death.

I studied it out in school and I studied it some more. When I was in high school I like to study corporal punishment, I did a paper on it. It is one of the most severe forms of capital punishment the world has ever known. The death by crucifixion did not come by being hung on the tree, or from the nails through the arms, wrist and the feet. Normally when one was crucified, it took upwards of three days to die. The person hung there. They had a little stand the feet were on, and as long as they could lift themselves up, they could breathe. Normally somewhere between the second and third day they were so physically exhausted that they could no longer stretch their body out, and allow their diaphragm to move, so they suffocated. That was the reason why the Roman soldiers were there at crucifixions. They were not there because the people were coming off the cross. They were there because family members would try to kill people hanging on the cross. Most often people went insane hanging on crosses. So, family members would try murdering them so they would not have to endure this. That's why the Roman soldiers came and broke the legs of the other two who were crucified with Jesus. Once their legs were broken they could no longer lift themselves up and they died. It was a horrible, horrible means of death.

I have always wondered, why the two men on the road to Emmaus, did not recognize Jesus, after His resurrection. Then, when I was meditating on this the Lord said, "Because His appearance was so marred, He was so physically beaten up, the lasting impression these men had of seeing Jesus hanging on the cross scarred their memory for life. When they saw the resurrected Christ, the resurrected Jesus, walking along healed and restored, they could not remember the Person they had known while they followed Him. For them the vision of Him hanging on the cross so scarred their memory they could not understand that."

The third thing God has used to help me stay free of this curse is the understanding of chastisement, God's chastisement. Hebrews Chapter 12:5-11 says, chastisement is something we need. If God does not chastise you, then you are a bastard. Chastisement is a very interesting word in the Greek. The Greek word for chastisement is *Paideia*. The literal Greek for *Paideia* means to train up a child. It is how the father would establish different ways for his son to grow up. If the father was a shop keeper, the father, when his son was young, would bring him in and has him sweep up, then it was restocking shelves, constantly bringing more and more responsibility into the son's life to cause him to grow up and mature, to walk in his father's trade.

Sons in those days usually took the trade of their fathers and stayed in it. Jesus' father was a carpenter and that is what Jesus grew up doing. If you were a shopkeeper you grew up as a shopkeeper. If you were a silversmith you grew up and learned the silversmith's trade. God wants us to understand that is the way He does it. He puts us in circumstances and situations to cause us to become like Him.

God establishes ways for us to grow up in His image. We do not have to worry about, "Well, am I doing enough to be like Christ?" God will make sure of it. He will place you in circumstances and situations that develop the Christ-like nature in your life, called character.

Character is learned in difficult times. Character is not learned in the soft paths of life. We have learned that submitting to the Will of God makes everything go a whole lot easier. When we first went to South

Carolina we went through a difficult time. We called Pastor up here and said, "Naomi, we have done it again." Her recommendation to us was, "Submit to them, even if it is not godly. Submit to your enemies. God will bring you through it. God will take care of you." We took that advice, with a great deal of difficulty; we found that God did marvelous things in our lives down there.

We need to embrace our circumstances. There are times in our lives that we need to deal with the enemy. We know the enemy comes in and tries to destroy us and to steal and to kill. That is true, but often I believe; a lot of what we go through, and experience, is done by the hand of God. The chastisement of God is meant to bring us to where He wants us to be. Paul says, "I've learned to be content in every situation and every circumstance." Let's learn to be content people.

God's chastisement is for our profit, that we might be partakers of His holiness. That is what it says in Hebrews 12, if we walk in holiness, there is no judgment. If there is no judgment, there is no curse. Embracing our chastisement Verses 12 and 13 of Hebrews 12, says, lifts us and brings us healing. What more can there be?

The fourth thing God showed me that I have had to use, to maintain this freedom, (to keep the ground that I have won back), is faith. This is the very first thing God told me when I read this pamphlet.

You must either believe it or you do not. If you do not believe it, there is no ground gained back. If you believe it, who knows what He will do for you! I cannot begin to tell you all of what He may do for you. We do not share the same circumstances; we do not share the same background. All I know is what has happened in our life. We are no one special we know that. If He did it for us, He will do it for anybody.

The very first thing that I heard from the enemy when I finished reading the pamphlet The curse of the Bastard was, what about Galatians 3:13. It says:

> **Galatians 3:13 (KJV)** *Christ hath redeemed us from the curse of the law, being made a curse for us: for it is written, cursed is every one that hangeth on a tree:*

I said, "Uh huh, yes that is true. Yes, I believe that." I began to think about it and realized what I heard was not healing. It was not part of the nature and character of what I know to be God. I began to wonder, "Who just said that to me?" I began to understand that it was Satan, the enemy that brought that Scripture to mind.

We need to learn something, Church. In this deliverance, I had to learn something. I have always considered the church as the father of legalism. The church is not the father of legalism. They have a "wonderful teacher" who has been round for years and his name is Satan.

It was Satan who came to Eve and said, "Did not God say to you that you shall not eat the fruit of this tree?" It was Satan who used the Word when he came to Jesus to tempt Him. He said, "This is the Word, isn't it?" He takes the literal translation of what was said and then he takes it and changes it, just slightly. That is what he did. He came up and said, "Sure Jesus broke the curse; there's no sense to believe that." He has already taken care of that.

I want to tell you what God told me. The law is still in effect, even today. Jesus Himself said, "I came not to destroy the law but to fulfill it." We do not live under the law; we live under grace and mercy. Satan knows the law is still in effect. He knows how to use it. He knows how to manipulate it and he knows how to manipulate us. It is the same with everything else. Jesus went to the cross and made salvation available to everybody. The one condition is to believe. If you do not believe it, you do not receive it. If you do, you are made sons and daughters of God. Healing was done the same way. Healing is part of the atonement. Unless we appropriate healing by faith, we walk around sick. We need to use faith to appropriate the healing that has already been provided. Faith comes by hearing, and hearing the Word of God. Curses still exist. There are so many more curses in the Word, other than just this one.

Satan uses them. God still uses them. That's right; the law exists because God still judges the world in accordance with the law. The primary law we have right now is to accept the cross. If you do not accept the cross, then you have judgment. You are ultimately going to go to hell. It is the same way in all the other areas of the law. They still exist. God uses the law to judge the world. We do not live that way, we live under grace and mercy but we still live in the world, we still are part of the world, we have come out of the world, the world is not totally out of us.

Israel wanted to go back to Egypt. We still like our little areas of Egypt. Little portions of Egypt still remain in us, at times. We need to use faith and say, "Okay I believe that, deliver me from Egypt. Take all of Egypt out to my life. Set me free, Lord."

The other thing that I have seen as part of this and I share it not so much as my own life because I did not understand it until recently. When God sets you free from curses it is a little bit different than just setting you free from demonic forces. Normally when I was set free from some type of demonic force I could sense immediately, something had happened. The changes were instantaneous. With this it was very subtle. I did not recognize for several weeks the freedom that came from being set free. It was probably close to a month before I really began to understand the changes that were taking place in my life. Jesus teaches us about the sower in Matthew 13:3-9 (KJV):

And he spake many things unto them in parables, saying, Behold, a sower went forth to sow; {4} And when he sowed, some seeds fell by the way side, and the fowls came and devoured them up: {5} Some fell upon stony places, where they had not much earth: and forthwith they sprung up, because they had no deepness of earth: {6} And when the sun was up, they were scorched; and because they had no root, they withered away. {7} and some fell among thorns; and the thorns sprung up, and choked them: {8} But other fell into good ground, and brought forth fruit, some a hundredfold, some sixtyfold, some thirtyfold. {9}, who hath ears to hear, let him hear. He explains this parable in Matthew 13:18-23 (KJV) Hear ye therefore the parable of the sower. {19} When any one heareth the word of the kingdom, and understandeth it not, then cometh the wicked one, and catcheth away that which was sown in his heart. This is he, which received seed by the way side. {20} But he that received the seed into stony places, the same is he that heareth the word, and anon with joy receiveth it; {21} Yet hath he not root in himself, but dureth for a while: for when tribulation or persecution ariseth because of the word, by and by he is offended. {22} He also that received seed among the thorns is he that heareth the word; and the care of this world, and the deceitfulness of riches, choke the word, and he becometh unfruitful. {23} But he that received seed into the good ground is he that heareth the word, and understandeth it; which also beareth fruit, and bringeth forth, some a hundredfold, some sixty, some thirty.

Jesus sows the Word in our life and the enemy comes to try and steal it. Cares of the world and deceitfulness of riches try to steal the Word. We need to exercise our patience along with our faith. Do not give your faith up just because tomorrow or the next day you do not see tremendous change.

I took a period to recognize the change. I am only now seeing things God's changed in my life. Exercise your patience along with your faith. Go through the Word. Patience and faith are always hooked up together. Hebrews 12 says that, so does James 1:3.

The sixth thing I have seen under this is John 8:2-11. It's the story of the woman who is brought to Jesus when she was caught in the act of adultery.

John 8:2-11 (KJV) And early in the morning he came again into the temple, and all the people came unto him; and he sat down, and taught them. {3} And the scribes and Pharisees brought unto him a woman taken in adultery; and when they had set her in the midst, {4} They say unto him, Master, this woman was taken in adultery, in the very act. {5} Now Moses in the law commanded us, that such should be stoned: but what sayest thou? {6} this they said, tempting him that they might have to accuse him. But Jesus stooped down, and with his finger wrote on the ground, as though he heard them not. {7} So when they continued asking him, he lifted up himself, and said unto them, He that is without sin among you, let him first cast a stone at her. {8} and again he stooped down, and wrote on the ground. {9} And they which heard it, being convicted by their own conscience, went out one by one, beginning at the eldest, even unto the last: and Jesus was left alone, and the woman standing in the midst. {10} When Jesus had lifted up himself, and saw none but the woman, he said unto her, Woman, where are those thine accusers? Hath no man condemned thee? {11} she said, No man, Lord. And Jesus said unto her, neither do I condemn thee: go, and sin no more.

Jesus said, "I do not condemn you. Just do one thing, go and sin no more." God has so specifically told me there are things I cannot do, just cannot do, because if I do I open myself to come under this curse. It may seem funny, it may seem strange, but that is the way it is. So, I say I will not do that because I do not want to live that way, anymore.

CHAPTER 8

Steps God Lead Me Through to Experience Freedom

HOW WAS I SET FREE? God gave me three very distinct steps. There is no formula for this. The only formula that I can give you is believe it, have faith in it. Believe what God said. God did show me three distinct steps that brought me to the point of freedom.

The first is one I have shared. I made a decision. I said, "I do not care what you require of me, just heal my mind!" For the most part I have been obedient to what God has asked me to do. We have endured some situations that I'd rather not have gone through. We still do. I would rather have been a lot of places than where I was the day I first taught this. That does not mean we are not content. When we were in England we were so envious of one of our friends back here. They had a house, they had a good job. We did not know how we were going to pay our rent. We did not know <u>where</u> our food was coming from.

It is not that way today. They're worse off in some way today than we were then. It has not been easy. While it's not gotten easier, it's gotten funnier! I love where I am at today.

Friedrich Nietzsche, and I do not promote Mr. Nietzsche, I do not particularly agree with a lot of his philosophies, but one thing he said, "What does not kill me, makes me better." That's true; I would not give up where we're at today for anything in the world! It just does not make any sense, anymore. The first thing was obedience.

The second was I decided in 1986 that there was no help for me outside of God. If God did not heal me I was going to remain this way the rest of my life. There is no other way. I said, "God you do it all or it will not get done." I put everything I had into trusting Him.

I must admit I gave up hope the summer of 1987. I totally gave up my hope. I was ready to walk away from everything. Not only walk away, like I shared, I was ready to kill myself because there was no hope left. That was the point God came in and did something.

When John Carr was at our church in October 1987, he shared a teaching on faith. It was the most profound, yet simplest teaching on faith I have ever heard. Balanced perfectly, it was the Word of the Lord. This was important because it was the week before or the week after that God began to minister to my life.

He shared one thing about faith out of Mark 11:22, 23 (KJV), concerning the passage about *"Say to this mountain be thou removed and be cast into the sea."* Anything that hinders God's purpose in our lives is a mountain and must be removed. Beloved, this curse was a mountain in my life! God said it had to be removed.

I do not claim that it was my great faith that believed God, and set all of this in motion. I have had too many people pray for me, for too many years. God used circumstances in our life to bring us to a particular point in our walk with Him, and in our faith life, and in our trust in Him. It was a mountain and it must be removed. It was not my faith. John Carr said it is God's faith; it is God's faith. It is God's gift to us. It is something that God says "Receive" and you just flow with that. I do not have to work up any great feelings. I do not feel the power of God going through my hand. It was His faith it was His faith.

CHAPTER 9

Setting Others Free from the Curse

I will close with one more thought. I began to look at some ways to set myself free, and to set other people free. God began to show me how to set someone else free from a curse. It is based on authority, and it is based on faith. Faith is based on authority. That is the teaching in Matthew 8:5-13. It is when the Roman centurion says, "Oh no, do not come, and I am a man under authority. I say to this one come and he comes, and to that one go and he goes." Jesus said, "I have never seen such faith in all of Israel." He (the centurion), says, "Do not come to my house, you do not have to do that, just speak the Word." The authority is in God's Word. Work with the authority that is all he told them. You have the authority to do that.

God has shown me that there are spheres of authority. That there are circles of authority, and they are based on covenant relationship.

1 Corinthians 7:14-16 (KJV) for the unbelieving husband is sanctified by the wife, and the unbelieving wife is sanctified by the husband: else were your children unclean; but now are they holy. {15} But if the unbelieving depart, let him depart. A brother or a sister is not under bondage in such cases: but God hath called us to peace. {16} for what knowest thou, O wife, whether thou shalt save thy husband? Or how knowest thou, O man,

127

whether thou shalt save thy wife?

One of the spheres He showed me was that I have authority over my own life. First and predominately, I exercise authority over my life. The second one is in the family; I exercise authority over my family. The third one is the authority over the church. We all know Jesus is Head over the church. One of the ways He demonstrates His authority is through the pastor over the church. If we submit to the pastor, it places us under God's authority through Jesus; it gives the pastor authority over our lives. It comes from submission, not to the authority that they walk in, but His authority that He placed in them. That gives a pastor right to exercise authority over our lives.

Then, He showed me a way to exercise authority over unbelievers, because I know there are families that have people who are under this, and who are not believers. He said there is a way we can exercise authority over unbelievers. That is love.

Jesus gained all authority by an act of love. God so loved the world that He gave. Jesus fulfilled that part of God's nature, His love nature, when He came and gave Himself as a sacrifice. He said to me, "If you are willing to pay the price and love them as I love them, if you are willing to pay the price to love them to wholeness, you can exercise authority to break curses over them.

He also gave me a very specific warning. Matthew 12:43-45 where it talks about binding the strong man and kicking him out.

Matthew 12:43-45 (KJV) When the unclean spirit is gone out of a man, he walketh through dry places, seeking rest, and findeth none. {44} Then he saith, I will return into my house from whence I came out; and when he is come, he findeth it empty, swept, and garnished. {45} then goeth he, and taketh with himself seven other spirits more wicked than himself, and they enter in and dwell there: and the last state of that man is worse than the first. Even so shall it be also unto this wicked generation.

You need to be careful, when he comes back and finds the place all swept and nice. He will respond, "This is a whole lot better than what I have." Again, my translation, "And he, (the demon), goes and brings seven others back with him. The last state of the man is worse than the first."

If you are not committed to love people to wholeness, be careful. It is too great of a possibility that someone will end up worse off. I pray you belong to a body of people who will love people to wholeness. We do not need to do it individually. We can do it together. That is why the church is in the world today.

In closing, I know I was an illegitimate child. I knew I was born as a bastard. You may not have that "privilege;" it may be a little more difficult for you to believe this. It is a curse that extends for 400 years. If anyone in your family for 400 years has had a bastard, an illegitimate child, some way or another, in your family linage that far back, how could you even have known the "private details of your family's lives?"

I believe there are not many people in the world that some time or another in the last 400 years of their family's life has not come under the curse of the Bastard. Like Solomon, it may not show up for years and years. It may never show up at all, I do not know. I am still learning much about this. Someplace or another I believe this affects all of us. I believe it affects men more than it does woman.

I believe personally, that the curse is the reason we see the struggle to see men saved, particularly in America. To struggle to see men walk in the fullness of what God has called them to do is directly related to this curse.

All the years I have walked as a Christian, since 1978, I have heard wives say, "Why doesn't my husband do this? Why doesn't he do that? What about my son? Why aren't the men interested in spiritual things?" Why aren't more of the men interested in spiritual things?

I have heard it everywhere we have gone. I think we have been under a curse. We want to do what we know is right but we cannot. The time has come, because God said so, that we will no longer live under this curse, unless we make it our decision to live under a curse.

PRAYER FOR DELIVERANCE
FROM THE CURSE OF THE BASTARD

Father, we come in the Name of Jesus. I bring every sin of our forefathers for 400 years up to You. I ask You to forgive this sin of bearing illegitimate children that is in my family line for 400 years. I ask You to forgive this sin that has displeased You, or if there has been anyone that has hated You and are bearing this iniquity, I ask you to forgive them also.

I know, Lord, that Your Word says that we bear the sins and the iniquities of our forefathers. And even though I am not illegitimate and have not committed sexual sins, I ask You to cleanse my blood line and anything that I have inherited from my forefathers.

I ask You, Jesus, to come with Your precious blood, with Your mighty hand and cleanse. Lord, clean out all of the old debris in me, that I know nothing about, and everything that hinders my growth as a Christian.

Lord, let Your precious anointing come upon me. Heal and cleanse by Your precious blood, by Your stripes that You bore. Lord, I claim healing. Because You hung on a tree and were made a curse, I do not have to bear this curse. Galatians 3:13 (KJV) says, Christ *hath redeemed us from the curse of the law, being made a curse for us: for it is written, Cursed is every one that hangeth on a tree:*

Lord, forgive me for all of my feelings of rejection, not being able to love people, not being able to really "enter in" and worship with a congregation, not ever feeling at home in any church.

I ask for Your help. I ask that this curse be lifted off me, (and my family).

Lord, I hate this enemy that works with this curse, making me feel like taking my life, making me feel rejected all the time, causing this sick feeling in my stomach.

Lord, put some pressure on that enemy by Your mighty hand, by Your Name, Jesus, by Your Word, and by Your Blood. Put pressure upon these evil powers and deliver me.

Lord, Your Word says, "Whoever calls on the Name of the Lord will be delivered." Lord, I call on You now. Deliver us from these spirits connected with the curse of the bastard, in the name of Jesus.

PRAYER FOR BLESSINGS AFTER DELIVERANCE FROM THE CURSE OF THE BASTARD

Now may the Lord Himself, bless you as you've been delivered from the curse of the bastard. May He heal every area that you've experienced rejection in. May you know God as the ultimate Father.

> *"For you did not receive the spirit of bondage again to fear, but you received the Spirit of adoption by whom we cry out, "Abba, Father.""* **Romans 8:15 NKJV**

May you be free of all feelings of suicide. May He make you to understand that you are not rejected, but loved and cherished. May you cleave to the Father as one. May all idolatry be put far away from you. May His peace free you from all anger. May His security replace all fear. May you ever know that you are held in the palm of His hand. May you know beyond a shadow of a doubt that you are wanted and cherished. May you always understand that you are His legitimate child. May you love with the same love you have received.

ABOUT THE AUTHOR

Jeff Hall was born in 1952 to an unwed 15-year-old girl. He was adopted as an infant; Jeff was raised in a home with two other sisters.

Raised in a Presbyterian Church, one of his earliest experiences was winning a Bible for memorizing the 23rd Psalm when he was in a 3rd grade Sunday School class.

Most of Jeff's early Christian experiences were centered around Sunday School and Vacation Bible schools.

In 1964, through the ministry of a friend of his adoptive mother, Jeff was born again and baptized in the Holy Spirit.

In High School, Jeff became involved with Camp Furthest Out, which was a non-denominational camp with an emphasis on going deeper into the "Spirit."

His Church involvement mostly revolved around whatever girlfriend that he was currently dating. In 1968 that was a girl whose family went to a Christian and Missionary Alliance Church. In 1969, he went to a Lutheran Church.

In 1969, at the age of seventeen, Jeff became a ward of the State of Michigan and ended up in a foster home.

After graduating from High School in 1970, Jeff worked for General Motors briefly before entering the U.S. Navy where Jeff received training in electronics, which launched a 20-year career in electronics.

Jeff married his High School girlfriend in 1971. They remained married for seven years before divorcing in 1978.

Jeff rededicated his life to the Lord in 1978 and has followed Jesus as His disciple since that time.

In 1978, Jeff met his current wife Libbie and while praying in tongues God told him to stop and interpret the tongue. The interpretation was that this woman, Libbie, was the women God had selected as his wife. Married in 1980, Jeff and Libbie will celebrate thirty-seven years of marriage in September of 2017. They have two grown children and five granddaughters.

Jeff and Libbie attended Harvest Bible College in Cornwall, England for a year. He finished a Bachelor of Arts in Christian Ministry from Indiana Christian University in 1994.

Jeff retired as an Information Technology (I.T.) Manager in 2008 after a twenty-two-year career in I.T.

Jeff has served as an Associate Pastor of Dwelling Place Ministries in Bay City, Michigan and is a teacher of the Bible.

Jeff has also been on short term mission's trips to the former Soviet Union and to Zambia. Jeff is Chairmen Emeritus of Revive Zambia, a group of local Zambian pastors seeking to bring revival to the nation of Zambia which he formed in 2016.

Jeff and Libbie currently worship at His House Church in Sturgis, Michigan.

Jeff may be contacted via email at: exalthisname@comcast.net